High Point

*A guide to walking the summits of
Great Britain's 85 historic counties*

VERTEBRATE **PUBLISHING**

Vertebrate Publishing, Sheffield.
www.v-publishing.co.uk

▲ HANGINGSTONE HILL, ROXBURGHSHIRE

High Point

A guide to walking the summits of
Great Britain's 85 historic counties

100,000 feet climbed
500 miles walked
One broken leg

Mark Clarke

To TL, who is just lovely

High Point

A guide to walking the summits of
Great Britain's 85 historic counties

 Copyright © 2014 Vertebrate Graphics Ltd and Mark Clarke.
Published in 2014 by Vertebrate Publishing.

Mark Clarke has asserted his right to be identified as the author of this Work.

ISBN: 978-1-910240-07-6

Cover photo: Snowdon summit trig point.   Photo: John Coefield.
Photography by Mark Clarke unless otherwise credited.

 All maps reproduced by permission of Ordnance Survey
on behalf of The Controller of Her Majesty's Stationery Office.
© Crown Copyright. 100025218
Design by Nathan Ryder, production by Rod Harrison – **www.v-graphics.co.uk**
Printed in China.

MIX
Paper from
responsible sources
FSC
www.fsc.org   **FSC® C016973**

Contents

▲ THE CHEVIOT, NORTHUMBERLAND

Introduction

The goal

In 2008 I set myself a goal: to visit all of Britain's counties, to have a good look around them and to stand on the highest point of each. In doing this I also wanted to learn more about the various counties and if possible to visit the county town of each. There were 85 counties to visit: 39 in England, 33 in Scotland and 13 in Wales. I had visited all but a handful of the counties before. All too often, I was just passing through on some motorway or dual carriageway without the time to gain any proper appreciation of them.

In retrospect it is hard to say exactly why I set myself the goal. Lots of factors were in play:

- I was impressed and inspired by David Dimbleby's *A Picture of Britain* TV series, in which Dimbleby pootled around the country in a battered old Land Rover. This seemed a very interesting thing to do and potentially a lot of fun.

- I had recently made a big life choice – to finish working 60-plus hours a week, which I had been doing for over 30 years, most recently as a finance director and previously as a management consultant, and to move to a less time-consuming portfolio career of non-executive roles in preparation for full retirement at some point in my sixties.

- I wanted to rebalance my life and spend more time in the rural parts of the country, rather than just in London and the other big cities, which had hitherto been the focus of my career.

- I also wanted to get out into the hills, which I had done little of since I was a teenager, when I had spent quite some time at school on expeditions in North Wales.

- I had had back trouble periodically ever since I slipped a disc about 30 years ago, and changes in the way I managed the condition meant my back was stronger and I could be more active.

I was prompted into action by my son Harry who – in 2002, when he was aged 12 – decided he wanted to go up Ben Nevis, and of course it would have to be me that took him up. Not knowing if I was actually fit enough to do this, we tested the water by going up Pen-y-ghent and Ingleborough in the Yorkshire Dales in 2002. This was successful and was followed up the following year with a walk up Snowdon. In 2006, by which time he had reached the age of 16, which seemed a decent necessary minimum if he were to do the climb, we scaled Ben Nevis – and very satisfying it was too. The significance for my later *High Point* ambitions was that it had convinced me that, if I could successfully tackle Ben Nevis, then I could reasonably expect to be able to take on any of the other high peaks that Britain has to offer.

So, early in 2008, I set myself the goal. I had climbed five of the high points before but I didn't know how long the rest would take – I assumed it would be several years, perhaps between five and ten.

Discovering the counties

At the time this was all a step into the unknown. The starting point was the counties: which were they and how many were there? I was already quite well acquainted with the English counties – at any rate I had heard of them all before, knew roughly where they were and knew a fair amount about each. But my knowledge of Wales was hazier, particularly regarding counties like Montgomeryshire and Brecknockshire. Where were they? What were they like? And Scotland was even more unknown – I discovered counties which I previously did not know existed, such as Wigtownshire, Clackmannanshire, Kirkcudbrightshire, Kincardineshire, and others too – Roxburghshire, Peebles-shire, Selkirkshire and Nairnshire; all were new to me.

Before long I discovered there were 85 'historic' counties – 39 in England, 33 in Scotland and 13 in Wales. These historic, or traditional, counties were the administrative areas of Britain prior to the sweeping changes brought in by the 1972 Local Government Act.

Their origins lie in the mists in British history. The country has been divided, categorised and split into areas since Roman times. In England, after the Romans left, a series of kingdoms were established which were gradually split into administrative shires (later counties) from the ninth century onwards. In Scotland, it was a series of sheriffdoms, introduced in the 12th century that formed for the basis of the historic counties, while in Wales, the Laws in Wales Act of 1535 abolished the existing system of rule, bringing the country under English Law and creating the historic counties in the process.

In 1972, the Local Government Act was passed after it was decided that the local government system needed to be restructured. It established a new system of county councils and, in doing so, abolished or merged several counties – particularly in Scotland – and re-drew the boundaries of many others. Familiar counties such as Flintshire, Rutland and all those referred to above disappeared and new county names came in – Avon, Tyne & Wear, Powys, and so on. This obviously caused confusion and, in some cases, upset among the inhabitants of those counties, who felt the loss of the county identity. (Many of the abolished counties still live on today in postal addresses, local papers and the regional identities.)

I decided to stick with the old historic counties, not least because they sounded more interesting and indeed historic – and 85 seemed a good number, quite a lot but hopefully not too many. I have since discovered on my travels that the old county names in fact have much resonance today and invariably feature quite proudly as districts within the newer, reorganised (and in Scotland and Wales usually much larger) counties.

The historic counties are extensively described in the much-derided, but actually hugely useful, Wikipedia internet-based encyclopaedia, which has several pages on each county and indeed on the towns within each county – covering such matters as the counties' geography, social and economic history and politics, plus information on transport, education and famous people. In short, a treasure trove of useful information, all freely available on the internet in a couple of mouse-clicks. Just reading these county descriptions has been very interesting, and indeed educational.

Then there was the question of the county high points – what and where were they? Wikipedia lists these, together with their Ordnance Survey grid references, and has easy click-through access to the Ordnance Survey website, where you can find the high point locations on online Ordnance Survey 1:25000 and 1:50000 maps by using their Get-a-Map facility.

All this was easier than I had expected but I had to exercise some care as in a few instances the Wikipedia high point information is wrong – I established this by triangulating with other sources on the internet. And I also had to ensure I was dealing consistently with the correct county definitions – as the high point of a historic county is not necessarily the high point of its modern equivalent with the same name. Two good examples are Lancashire and Yorkshire. Their historical high points are Old Man of Coniston (p148) and Mickle Fell (p254) respectively, whereas under modern definitions they are Gragareth and Whernside (p257) – I decided to climb all four!

What's more, in some counties the actual heights of some of the high point contenders have been in dispute – for example in Wiltshire, where some think Milk Hill is the highest and others Tan Hill. These definitional matters can get a bit technical and tedious, so I decided the best thing was to just weigh up such evidence as presented itself and then to take a view, aligning with what appeared to be the consensus.

The seemingly simple but necessary initial task of identifying the British counties and their high points made me realise how little I really knew about Britain's counties. Although I thought I had a good knowledge of British geography, I soon discovered I knew a lot less than I thought. About 90 per cent of the high point names were new to me. This was quite instructive, although I didn't realise it much at the time, as countless learnings and pleasant little surprises awaited me on my travels later on. Indeed, it is these which have made my *High Point* quest so interesting and fun to pursue, and such a treat to experience and discover.

Visiting the tops

So, with five of the 85 high points already bagged in previous years, I set out in June 2008 to bag the rest. I started with Wiltshire (Milk Hill) and by the end of June had visited six more – all easy ones in the Home Counties.

This encouraged me to continue and by the end of 2008 I had reached 33, the last one being the somehow appropriately named Boring Field in Huntingdonshire. Boring Field has the distinction of being, at 262 feet, the lowest of all the county high points. In 2008 I also visited Britain's lowest point, Holme Fen (minus nine feet) in Huntingdonshire, about 15 kilometres south of Peterborough.

All of my trips in 2008 were in England and Wales, so I determined in 2009 to make serious inroads into the Scottish hills. By the end of 2009, a further 20 had been added and my total had reached 58, including 12 counties in Scotland and the three biggest beasts on my list after Ben Nevis – Ben Macdui (4,295 feet, the high point of both Aberdeenshire and Banffshire), Ben Lawers (3,983 feet, in Perthshire) and Carn Eige (3,881 feet, in Ross-shire and Cromarty-shire). By the end of 2010, 20 more were climbed and my total stood at 78.

In 2011 I climbed eight more, before curtailing my activities for that year in August after breaking my leg in a horrible crisis on the remote moorland of Renfrewshire's Hill of Stake – on my own, miles from anywhere and anyone, in the mist and without a mobile phone signal. This was hugely disappointing as I only had three to go and had planned to complete the full set of all counties just a few weeks later in October 2011.

2012 was a difficult time, as it was quite a struggle to get my get leg back to normal, and on many occasions I thought it would not be possible to finish the last three climbs. However, on 15 August 2012, I happily stood on Aran Fawddwy in Merioneth and completed my quest.

In the end, I drew stumps at 89 tops, being the 85 which I had intended at the outset plus four more – Gragareth and Whernside (the high points on the new definitions for Lancashire and Yorkshire respectively), Cauldcleuch Head (the high point of Roxburghshire on the Wikipedia definition, which I subsequently discovered was wrong – the correct one is Hangingstone Hill in the Cheviot hills), and An Cliseam (the high point of the Western Isles, which now have county status although historically they were split as between Ross and Cromarty and Inverness-shire).

By the end, in August 2012, I was widely travelled. I had climbed over 100,000 feet and walked almost 500 miles. I had driven over 15,000 miles and hired 23 cars. I had been on 28 trains and travelled over 8,000 miles in them. I had flown on 23 aeroplanes for about 12,000 miles, and stayed in 74 B&Bs. All this in 54 trips from my home in London.

It had all been the most fantastic treat, adventure and indeed education.

Acknowledgements

In publishing this book I particularly want to record my gratitude to the following:

To my wife Alex for her unwavering total support and enthusiasm throughout, notwithstanding the project's long timescale, expense, bizarre nature and various travails – particularly after my accident on the Hill of Stake.

To Lesley Bryce (who is a professional mountain guide based in Ayrshire), who accompanied me up the Hill of Stake at the successful third attempt. It was good of her to agree at short notice to go with me on my July 2012 walk and I am most grateful for her assistance that day, which was a big one for me as my head was still full of memories of my disastrous attempt the previous summer.

To Jon Barton of Vertebrate Publishing for agreeing to publish the book and for the expertise which Jon and his colleagues, particularly John Coefield and Tom Fenton, showed in compiling and editing the book.

▲ LOOKING NORTH FROM THE OLD MAN OF CONISTON TOWARDS SCAFELL PIKE.

▲ KINDER SCOUT, DERBYSHIRE

BY: JOHN COEFIELD

The journey, on reflection

This project has been the most fantastic treat, adventure and indeed education – easily the best project I have ever done, appealing at so many different levels and in so many different ways.

High points as a metaphor
The fascination of my project has been not so much the standing on the county high points themselves, rewarding though that has always been – particularly when the route to them has been tough, but more the journey to the high point, the trips around the counties and the discoveries unexpectedly made along the way. So my *High Point* project has almost become a metaphor for the excitement and the learning I experience on journeys into the (comparative) unknown and in doing new things.

The countless surprises
When you make a journey like this you enjoy countless surprises which bubble up on each trip; you continually discover new things, frequently almost by chance. These are things which are not easily found in books or on the Internet, but are things which you can only readily discover and appreciate by browsing about in person – in my case on the journey around the county and up its high point. Many are small or quirky local things, others are better known and/or significant – but pretty well all of them are somehow surprising and interesting to discover.

Living as I do in London I find its metropolitan and cosmopolitan culture to be truly a world away from what I experienced on most of my travels. So for much of the time it has felt like being in another country – very interesting and refreshing.

Pioneering spirit
There are many people (over 5,000 I believe) in this country who have bagged all the Munros and also many who bag Corbetts, Grahams and Marilyns too. But very few seem to have been to the high point of all the counties in Britain. For more than two years I thought I might be the first, then in autumn 2010 I accidentally discovered via the Internet someone who had finished around the time I was starting in 2008. I think I am probably the second – who knows, perhaps there are others. In any event it is fun to do things which are new or innovative.

The remoteness
Almost all of the high points are, in the context of the counties they are in, in quite remote spots, sometimes very much so. Not much is built in this country above 1,000 feet or so (Britain's highest village, Flash in Staffordshire, is 1,519 feet above sea level) and about three quarters of the high points I visited were above this level. Most high points have no trees

nearby for miles. In several cases there is no road within five miles. Not only are the high points physically remote, many are also little visited – on almost all my walks to the high points over 1,500 feet (other than in the honeypots such as Ben Nevis, Snowdon and Helvellyn) I saw less than a handful of people all day; on many I saw no one for five or six hours.

This remoteness is both hugely appealing to experience, particularly the quietness when city life is so crowded and noisy, but it has its risks too, particularly if you are on your own and your mobile phone has no signal. Hence the need to avoid accidents and injury, and to prepare well.

The flora and fauna

I neither understand nor recognise (sufficient to name) most of the flora and fauna which I encountered on my journeys, nor did I take the trouble to learn about them, which I now regret. Notwithstanding this, it was always a treat to see the lovely, kaleidoscopic colours on display and the huge range of flora and fauna which is everywhere when you are off the beaten track. Nicest were perhaps the multi-coloured lichens on rocks and the deeply coloured plants on moorland, particularly after rain. I also had a pleasant surprise a couple of times coming across mountain hares and eagles.

The vistas

When weather permitted, the vistas around me were frequently superb. The best examples were from Ben More Assynt, Carn Eige, Ben Lawers, Bidean nam Bian, Ben Macdui and Goatfell. But there were countless memorable lower-level vistas too, for example from Kinder Scout, Shining Tor, Pen y Fan and Whitehorse Hill.

Exploring the counties

A key part of the project was to explore each county. The high point walks met that objective in a particular way, but spending a day or two, sometimes more, in each county visiting various towns and villages, as well as local shops, cafes and sundry places of interest was both interesting and fun. The variety in the various 'sundry places of interest' was astonishing, encompassing such places as the Boston Stump, the Mappa Mundi in Hereford, the Great Glasshouse at the National Botanic Gardens of Wales, Skara Brae on Orkney, the Lyness World War II museum on Hoy, the Muckle Roe and Eshaness coastlines on Shetland, the beaches on Harris, Loch Affric in Ross-shire and Cromartyshire, the Castle of Mey and Lybster in Caithness, the windmill at Holbeach, Ruskin's house in Coniston, and so on.

The sheer beauty of the countryside

Neither words nor photos can satisfactorily convey the incredible beauty of Britain's countryside. It doesn't matter where you go in Britain – if you are away from the roads and get off the beaten track, you will almost always find you are in a lovely spot. This beauty changes with height – the higher you go, the more elemental the beauty becomes. A switch seems to flip around the 3,000 feet level (sometimes lower), and above this the landscape becomes more barren, bleak, basic and windswept; greens become more brown, greys become more prominent, vegetation less obvious, trees non-existent.

The countryside's variety

The variety in Britain's countryside is astonishing, surely as great as in any other country. The hills, the valleys, the moorland, the peat bogs, the farmland, the stone walls, the stony beaches, the sandy beaches, the pastures, the streams, the rivers, the cows, the sheep, the heather, the gorse, the craggy hills, the houses, the market towns, the villages, the hamlets, the quirky little fields, the mega fields for agribusiness, the hedgerows, the flowers, and so on. And yes, the blots on the landscape too. Fantastic, unbeatable variety, and all pretty well on our doorstep.

Market towns

Small, and not so small, market towns used to be the backbone of this country, but that all changed with the growth of cities. And when you travel around the country on motorways and dual carriageways you tend not to see them. One of my project's treats has been to visit so many lovely market towns, both the small ones and the central parts of the larger ones.

The walks

Except in four cases – Norfolk, Suffolk, Huntingdonshire and Nottinghamshire – where the high points are actually on a road, the walks were all interesting in one way or another, even those whose prospects at the start seemed least. And even those high points which were the easiest to walk to – Cleeve Hill in Gloucestershire, Ebrington Hill in Warwickshire, Betsom's Hill in Kent – were all appealing in some way. Perhaps it was through the knowledge that the high point (in being the high point) was somehow special, or conversely that they were totally unremarkable, in a strange way made them appealing in a British sort of way.

Reaching the top

I always found reaching a high point strangely rewarding. Another milestone achieved, progress towards my greater goal, the pleasure of knowing the hard bit is over, the satisfaction of success, the comfort of knowing exactly where I was (when it had sometimes previously been less certain than I would like!), the relief of knowing I could send a text announcing I was on top, a nice buzz.

The honey search

My idea of seeking to bring back local honey (p26) from each county gave, somewhat surprisingly, an excellent boost to my desire to explore counties more widely and to dig around in places which I might not otherwise go to. Finding local honey was often quite hard and my search took me to all manner of butchers (who to my surprise often sell honey), bakers, cheese shops, greengrocers, fishmongers, farm shops, health food shops, delicatessens, cafes and market stalls. This also helped me to focus on many villages and small towns which I might not otherwise have visited.

Local delicacies

As I've travelled around, it's been fun to happen on local food specialities and treats. For example, the ice cream sundaes at Nardini's in Largs, the chutneys and marmalade from Trengilly Wartha in Cornwall and the Stagg Inn in Herefordshire, the mussels in Shetland, the seafood in Wester Ross, the many local beers throughout England (but not Scotland, where the beer is for some reason not so good), the Labrador-sized bread in Sherborne, the teas at Betty's in Yorkshire, the local cheeses, the malt whiskies in Scotland, the home-made cakes in countless cafes, and of course the local honeys.

Village names

Place names are a continual joy to discover when travelling round England, particularly in southern England where the names (particularly the double barrelled names) seem much more fun and quintessentially English than elsewhere – names such as: Blandford Forum, Sturminster Newton, Shepton Mallett, Hinton St George, Moreton-in-Marsh, Stoke Poges, Guiting Power, Aston Clinton, Toot Baldon, Great Tew, Bury St Edmonds, Burnham Thorpe, Brancaster Staithe, Melton Mowbray, Henley in Arden, Bovey Tracey, Corton Denham and countless others.

Scottish place names have their interest too, names such as Auchtermuchty, Auchterarder, Ardnamurchan, Altnaharra, Achnasheen, and Aulannakalgach (where my wife Alex's great great great great grandmother lived 200 years ago) – strangely, all names that start with an A. These A names all somehow inspire the imagination towards matters Scottish but, surprisingly, the places themselves did not always live up to my high expectations.

Somewhat bizarrely and amusingly, many Scottish place names have an almost pompous-seeming emphasis on avoiding the use of apostrophes – as in Ring of Brodgar, Broch of Durness, Water of Leith, Castle of Mey, Kyle of Lochalsh, Hill of Stake, Boat of Garten, Bridge of Urr, Pass of Drumochter, and countless others all round Scotland. My favourites are Yetts o' Muckart in Kinross-shire and Neive of the Spit (which is on Merrick, Kirkcudbrightshire's high point). This oddity extends to people's names too – even one of my honey jars is from (presumably Mr) Hood of Ormiston.

And then there is Assynt, Suilven, Brora, Muckle Roe, Esha Ness, Skara Brae, Uist, Pitlochry, Killiecrankie, Hoy, Morven, Flotta, Luskentyre, Taransay, Scarista, Benbecula, and especially Tillicoultry – all of which seem to convey something extra.

Scotland

I give Scotland, which I visited over 20 times, a special mention as it has many fantastic assets and special charms: its mountains, glens, coast, lochs, islands, rivers, heritage, whisky, produce (seafood, fish, beef, cheese, soft fruit), fishing, shooting, golf, and its fresh, unpolluted air. And Edinburgh, which is a superb, cultured city, wonderfully captured in the 2010 film *The Illusionist*, which is set in the fifties.

These assets are a compelling mix and compare well to any country in the world. Wester Ross, Assynt, the Western Isles, Orkney and Shetland are particularly special places – they are also pleasantly unvisited, so people seemingly do not much recognise their huge charms. The special flavour of Scotland is somehow captured excellently in the delightfully haunting (seemingly Scottish but actually American) lament *Ashokan Farewell* and in the atmospheric film *Local Hero*.

Sleuthing

As some 90 per cent of the mountains and hills which I climbed were previously unknown to me, and in hidden-away parts of the country which I had not been to before, substantial sleuthing was needed in getting to the high point: working out what the high point was, where it was, how best to get to it, what was interesting in its neighbourhood and county, where to stay, where to eat. All a bit like putting a jigsaw puzzle together.

Getting there

The trip to each high point always had its particular purpose, and inching towards that aim always had the strange appeal of a countdown when you know the end is in sight.

Planning and doing the project

A project like this requires a huge amount of planning, organising, determination and activity-completion, all of which play to some of my skill-sets. So just doing these things was of personal interest.

The sense of achievement

As this project has taken so long to complete, and with such a need for commitment and persistence, and seen in so many people's eyes as quite innovative, it feels a real achievement to have completed it. Indeed it is very rewarding. The range and depth of what has appealed about my high point project has been huge – these are the pluses, and there have been very many.

But what of the minuses?

The worst minus has been spending so much time on my own away from home. 25 of my 54 trips were on my own, and 49 (including most of my Scottish ones) of my 89 walks. You get used to it of course, indeed it's to an extent inevitable on a project such as this, but that doesn't mean it's not a minus.

On the more serious walks it can be quite forbidding when setting out on your own knowing there will be tricky bits of some kind ahead or that some accident might occur – notwith-standing the relief afterwards when all turned out to be well.

Nor have I enjoyed the winter layoffs, necessary though they have been due to the risks of winter mountain walking and short daylight hours seeming a bridge too far.

My personal need for a few days recovery time after the more significant walks was also an irritant, but only because it slowed me up in completing the project and meant I had to make more trips.

Some of the project's transport and accommodation practicalities had their dark side – the (periodically uncomfortable) beds in some B&Bs, my discomfort in many of the (small and therefore less expensive) rental cars which I hired, and also my preference not to travel on the Virgin West Coast rail line (cramped, claustrophobic carriages and tilting mechanisms which cause discomfort, at any rate for me).

Also, the project required a lot of persistence – four years, 54 trips, 85 counties is not for everyone! That said, a similar project would be quite doable for many people, involving just a dozen or so trips a year.

And finally, of course the cost of the project has been quite significant. With so many trips and 35,000 miles travelled it could not be otherwise.

But, it's all been worth it – just wonderful.

▲ SNOWDON FROM NEAR THE TOP OF THE PYG TRACK

BY: JOHN COEFIELD

The hairiest moments

In a project like this, which visits such remote locations, occasional mishaps are inevitable. Here are three I experienced during my travels ...

Hill of Stake (Renfrewshire)

Top of the hairy list, by miles, has to be the disaster which I had to cope with, and indeed overcome, on the Hill of Stake, Renfrewshire's high point.

In advance, it seemed that the strangely-named Hill of Stake would be a reasonably straightforward high point to negotiate, albeit one in quite a remote location: moderate in height (1,713 feet), just a mile or so over moorland from a decent miners' track, in the heart of the Clyde Muirshiel Regional Park. But, in practice, the walk turned into a struggle for survival.

I arranged my trip on the basis of a good weather forecast the day before, but when I arrived at the start, the park's (closed) visitor centre, it was raining heavily.

I set out in any case as the start of the walk was very straightforward, an old miners' track for some three miles up to disused barytes mines, intending to reconsider when I reached the mines. From there it would be about a mile over open moorland, with no path, to the top.

When I reached the mines, the weather had eased and I could see the way to the top – easy enough, albeit very heathery and boggy. I set off.

Half an hour later, with about 400 metres to go, a thick mist fell. If I were to continue, it would have to be on a compass bearing over featureless terrain with my target destination hard to distinguish in the mist – it seemed risky, so I decided to turn back, somewhat irritated to miss out on the high point.

A minute or so later disaster struck. As I was walking, my right boot plummeted into an invisible hole, up to my knee and I instinctively stamped my left foot out to stabilise myself; I heard a couple of cracks and immediately thought the ankle must have broken. Even worse, it seemed for a moment something similar might have happened to the right leg – in which case I would be immobilised. A horrendous situation – on my own, miles from anywhere, on boggy moorland with no one else on the hills, away from mobile signal, and in thick mist. The classic mountain nightmare scenario.

Fortunately, the right leg was OK – but I could barely put any weight on my left leg and every step was a struggle on the rough terrain. The only tenable option was to attempt to get off the moorland and head on a compass bearing back to the old mine workings, where I hoped to find other people – or a mobile signal so I could call for help.

Some time and a mile or so later, I reached the mine and luckily found a mobile signal, so was able to call home some 400 miles away – a massive relief, although I was very conscious of the instant worry it would create at the other end.

I then limped the three miles on the miners' track back to my start point, dipping out of mobile signal as I did so. When I got back to base I discovered, somewhat to my surprise, I could just use my car's clutch pedal with my gammy foot so drove off a few miles back to safety.

All the while after the break, I of course entertained horrible fears of how bad the ankle injury might be, whether nasty permanent damage had been done, whether the injury might somehow cause uncontrollable internal bleeding, or whether I might be overwhelmed and go into serious shock. In the event, the damage turned out to be a broken fibula just above the ankle in my leg, which took five months to fix – six weeks immobilised in plaster, then three weeks in an Aircast boot, then three months of physiotherapy and hydrotherapy to rebuild my muscles and get back to some kind of normal movement – recovery was far harder than I had imagined it might be, both physically and mentally. The hospital consultant was amazed that my three mile walk had been possible and that more damage hadn't been done.

In the event, a happy enough ending in the circumstances, but a major scare and certainly one of the worst experiences in my life. Quite a lucky escape.

11 months later, on 20 July 2012, I revisited the Hill of Stake and climbed it successfully.

Mickle Fell (Yorkshire)

Second on my list is Mickle Fell. This has a certain notoriety as it is on Ministry of Defence land and access to it is heavily restricted (to about two days per month) and contingent on access permits from the MoD establishment at nearby Warcop. So there was always the fear that I might tread on an unexploded shell!

However, it was three other factors which were a more serious concern – thunder and lightning, a torrent to cross, and Mickle Fell's remoteness.

I started my walk at Hilton, which is some eight miles from the summit. In any case the day would be a long one.

The first half of the ascent up Scardale was straightforward enough, albeit wet, taking me to the valley head some 2,000 feet up. From there it was a four-mile walk across remote moorland (heather, bogs, peat hags) – flat then steadily up, with no human habitation in sight. This was heavy going and by the time I reached the top I feared that the return route solo across the moors would be a bit risky on account of the remoteness (away from mobile signal), the heaviness of the terrain (making the distance hard work) and the difficulty in finding the route if the mist came down (which seemed quite likely).

Then, when I reached the top, there was a big clap of thunder and lightning, with seemingly potential for more.

Not a good place to be, and nowhere to take shelter. To be struck by lightning up there would be awful, potentially terminal. As luck would have it, I met two others (Glen and Otis, Corbett-baggers and the only two people I saw all day) on top, so I asked if I could join them on their descent – they happily agreed to this, but the consequence was that I would have to finish 10 miles as the crow flies (and 30 miles by road) from my start in Hilton. But that was a problem for later – solved by Glen kindly driving me later on to Middleton-in-Teesdale, where I got an expensive taxi back to Hilton.

However, the biggest consequence was unforeseen – in taking the return route we had to cross Maize Beck. My companions had found this straightforward a couple of hours previously, but the beck had risen in the rain and swelled into rapids which were difficult to cross safely, never mind without getting wet. It took us some time to find a suitable crossing point – where the (previously beck, now) river was some 20 metres wide. The river was fast flowing and rising while we deliberated.

In the end we had to wade through the in-places waist high river, struggling to stay upright, without falling over the boulders on the riverbed. To facilitate this, Otis and I crossed together, holding on to each other in a square formation with both arms. A difficult, tense crossing! We then had to walk, wet through, for three miles past Cauldron Snout and back to their car.

Mickle Fell – by no means the highest of my high points, but that day probably the toughest.

Carn a Ghille Chearr (Morayshire)

My walk up Carn a Ghille Chearr was notable as I got lost in mist and a blizzard on the summit. When I set off on the walk, the tops of the Cromdale hills were hidden by clouds which sat about 500 feet below the summit. Shortly after I entered the clouds it started snowing. There wasn't a footpath but the route to the summit seemed straightforward , and indeed it proved to be so. However, while I was walking the snow was settling – just a couple of inches but enough to cause, together with the mist, a white-out sensation.

So to return, I set off on a compass bearing, aiming to retrace my route on the way up. This was tricky as the one kilometre route from the summit to Carn Eachie was a flattish wide convex-shaped grassy ridge without distinguishing features. About 15 minutes from leaving the top I was surprised to come across four cairns right next to each other, which I had not seen on the way up. Nor were they on the map.

This was somewhat confusing, but I was even more confused 15 minutes later to find myself back at the top. Quite alarming – I had spent the previous 30 minutes going full circle and not realised it. In view of the conditions (mist, blizzard) I decided I had to exit the mountain to below cloud level straight away – I headed downhill on a south-east bearing off to safety.

Getting lost in this way had been an object lesson in how tricky it can be to follow a bearing on your own, even if you are being very careful and following the correct procedures, in quite featureless white-out conditions.

A final word

These incidents, and also the more minor ones referred to elsewhere in this book, serve as a good reminder of the need to be mindful of the risks which one faces when walking in the hills – particularly of the need to be properly prepared for the walk, to make suitable judgements during it (balancing risk with other factors), to have the right equipment and clothing, and to have a good detailed map (Ordnance Survey 1:25,000 scale is best) and compass – and to know how to use them properly. Other considerations are set out in the Walking in the Hills chapter (p31).

The Honey Project

After visiting a few counties, it occurred to me that it would be nice to bring something home from each one – a souvenir, something individual or memorable. But what? I decided it had to be something made in the county.

Rather than accumulate a heap of items, such as local arts and crafts, which I did not need, I thought the best thing would be to bring back something consumable, but which would not perish too quickly. It also had to fit into a suitcase. That ruled out fruit, vegetables and the like. It seemed best to bring back a jar of something; I presumed it would be possible to locate locally made chutneys or jams in each county, but I didn't want 85 jars of pickle – how would I eat all that?!

I wondered if honey might be the answer. I have toast and honey each day for breakfast. Perhaps I could find local honey in each county and it might be a tastier product than I usually ate – as, for example, malt whisky is to blended whisky?

I decided to see if I could buy local honey from each county that I visited. This was easier than first thought, and, before long, my cupboard at home filled up with honey jars faster than I could eat them.

First I had 10 jars in my cupboard, then 20, then 30 – when would the pile stop growing? Thankfully, my stock of honey jars rose and fell on an annual cycle. The jar count rose during the spring to autumn walking season as I visited the counties and then fell in the winter months, as I ate the honey which I had accumulated throughout the year. At its height the stock reached about 50 jars, but fortunately subsided as I ate; as I write the jar count is about 20, down from its peak, but it will still take me a year to eat.

The pursuit of local honey took me to all sorts of places I would not otherwise have visited – local butchers often stock local honey, as do some bakers, cheese shops, farm shops, green grocers, delicatessens, market stalls and health food shops. I even found a jar in a museum shop (in Bewdley) and a tourist information shop (in Berwick-upon-Tweed). But never in supermarkets – almost none of my jars have bar codes. This made me a more active observer of the places I visited and I found that the deeper I sleuthed to seek out the honey, the more I noted what was in the town or village I was visiting.

The production of local honey in this country is very much a cottage industry, actually a cottage industry par excellence. One of the little quirks of this is the producers' attitudes to 'eat before' dates. Pretty well all the jars (but not all) have eat before dates (month and year) stamped or written on them – so far so good. However, some set dates within the next year or so, others within two years, and others at more distant dates – the most distant date I have come across is about 10 years away. From this I conclude that most dates must be all but irrelevant.

Somewhat to my surprise, and without undue effort but necessarily with some persistence, I have been able to find local honey in almost all of the British counties – I have only failed in eight counties, all in Scotland: Selkirkshire, Peebles-shire, Kinross-shire, Clackmannanshire, West Lothian, Dunbartonshire, Bute and Wigtownshire. This at a time when the media says this country is low on honey.

Pricing policies were frequently baffling – the average price of a pound jar was in the range of £4 to £5, the lowest price being £2.71 and the highest over £12 (which I did not buy …). Clearly, most suppliers of local honey keep their bees and sell their honey as a hobby rather than as a primary source of income, and few can have any expectation of making much money from it, except presumably in the more industrial scale operations.

The cottage industry dimension shines through on the labels on the jars – in many cases you can almost feel the supplier's pride stand out from their labels. Whilst some suppliers simply base their labels on a standard commercially available template, many have created something special, with attractive and quite artistic photographic and lithographic work – most notably the Northamptonshire honey with a picture of a local church in snow, or the Bedfordshire one with a picture of a hawthorn bush in blossom. Some are rather fun, as with the Warwickshire one from Stratford-upon-Avon which included a print of Shakespeare's head. One, bought at a farm shop in Flintshire, had no label at all.

Whilst local honey in England invariably trumpets the county which it is from, this is much less the case in Scotland, where suppliers typically prefer to say their honey is 'Scottish' – a sort of anti-localism which presumably would be anathema to the suppliers of, say, 'Regents Park honey' in London or 'Presteigne honey' in Radnorshire.

Even the jars were not without their interest. In England the honey comes in one-pound (454-gram) or sometimes three-quarter-pound (340-gram) jars. However, in Scotland it is frequently sold in half-pound (227-gram) jars – but at the full one-pound price which you usually pay elsewhere. The smallest jar which I bought was a quarter-pound jar in Cornwall.

I also found the diversity of the honey which I obtained to be surprisingly broad, with every shade of colour in set honey from dark brown (heather honey) to almost white; and every type of consistency from smooth and creamy through to crystalline or almost rock hard. I always opted for set honey rather than runny honey, if there was a choice, as that is, in my opinion, tastier on bread. However, I also came away with a fair amount of runny honey as that is handy for cooking. Most of all though, all the honeys I have bought have been very tasty, a pleasure at the breakfast table and always a nice little reminder of where I have visited.

▲ 100 BRITISH HONEYS – DESIGN BY MARK CLARKE FROM JARS PURCHASED THROUGHOUT BRITAIN

Bests, worsts, mosts, leasts

Counties

Biggest: Yorkshire	An area of 12,000 square kilometres (3 million acres), comfortably the largest county in Britain. Inverness-shire is the next largest.
Smallest: Clackmannanshire	An area of just 160 square kilometres, less than half the size of Rutland.
Most liked: Shetland, Orkney, & the Western Isles	Just delightful, with a strong island feel, and unlike anywhere else in Britain.
Yorkshire	Lovely countryside and villages, huge variety and a special character. God's Country.
Least liked: Renfrewshire	Too closely associated with my ill-fated exploits on the Hill of Stake.
Most surprising: Shetland	Number 6 in Lonely Planet's 2011 Top 10 regions, and justly so. A huge treat and constant delight, with amazing natural scenery and birdlife.

High points

Highest point: Ben Nevis (Inverness-shire)	A 4,409-feet hulk, towering over Loch Linnhe below.
Lowest point: Holme Fen (Huntingdonshire)	9 feet below sea level!
Lowest high point: Boring Field (Huntingdonshire)	At only 262 feet, easily the lowest county top.
High point on a road: Huntingdonshire, Norfolk, Nottinghamshire, Suffolk.	
Best view from top: Ben More Assynt (Sutherland)	Views right across northern Scotland, with the Moray Firth glinting in the sun over 50 miles away.
Carn Eige (Ross & Cromarty) & Ben Lawers (Perthshire)	Unforgettable views of countless peaks in all directions under beautiful clear blue skies.
Most northerly: Ronas Hill (Shetland)	
Most southerly: Brown Willy (Cornwall)	
Most remote: Morven (Caithness)	In Caithness's Flow Country, a 4,000-square-kilometre wilderness and Europe's largest expanse of blanket peat bog.

Walks

Most liked: Carn Eige (Ross & Cromarty)	An unforgettable Highlands walk on a lovely day, with a dozen Munros nearby and starting in Glen Affric, which is a little known gem.
Least liked: Hill of Stake (Renfrewshire)	Tussocky, lumpy terrain with many hidden (and dangerous!) foot-sized holes.
Toughest: Mickle Fell (Yorkshire)	Survived lightning and crossed a raging torrent on a long, hard wet walk over heavy terrain.
Easiest: Ebrington Hill (Warwickshire)	Just 200 metres walk from the car.
Hottest: Milk Hill (Wiltshire)	30°C during the walk.
Coldest: Ben Cleuch (Clackmannanshire)	A foot of snow at the top and biting winds.
Windiest: Morven (Caithness)	I was unable to stand in a gale at the top for fear of being blown over the nearby cliff edge.
Wettest: Fan Foel (Carmarthenshire)	Heavy rain all day for five hours from start to finish.
Riskiest: Hill of Stake (Renfrewshire)	Terrain with many invisible holes underfoot.
Most memorable walks: Ben More Assynt (Sutherland)	A tough walk, wonderful views and surrounded by ghosts of my wife's Assynt ancestors.
Ben Nevis (Inverness-shire)	Climbing Ben Nevis gave me the confidence to undertake my *High Point* project.
Ben Lomond (Stirlingshire)	My son Harry's first Munro, when aged 12.
West Cairn Hill (West Lothian)	A winter wonderland of snow under a cloudless blue sky.
Ward Hill (Orkney)	Stunning views over Scapa Flow. Avoided the bonxies' kamikaze antics!
Bidean nam Bian (Argyll)	A big beast towering high above Glencoe.
Aran Fawddwy (Merioneth)	Special as it was my final walk of the *High Point* project.

Walking in the hills

I found that good planning before each trip paid off greatly. Walking a good route, choosing suitable kit, finding good accommodation, paying reasonable costs for travel, indeed doing the walk at all – all are easier if you plan early.

Access to three high points is restricted at certain times of the year – at High Willhays in Devon and on Mickle Fell in Yorkshire this is due to Ministry of Defence activity. Be sure to check with the MoD for restrictions before setting out. At Morven in Caithness the restriction is due to deer culling activity. Use the Hillphones service or the new Heading for the Scottish Hills website for information before setting out. It's best not to discover these restrictions at the last minute (as I did on High Willhays).

Timing matters. In winter the days are short (which means less time for walking) and the weather is colder, snowier and wilder – tricky if you are on your own – and consequently I avoided the winter months (November to February) during my project. There is also still quite a lot of snow on the hills in Scotland in March and April, which is not my cup of tea.

Rail and air fares are also very time sensitive, so advance planning helps. And there are far fewer people, often seemingly nobody, on the hills during the week. Accommodation is generally both cheaper and less in demand outside the weekends. Doing the walks midweek is often really worthwhile.

On many walks it helps hugely to know what **weather** to expect, even if the actual weather turns out – as is often the case in the UK – to be different from the forecast. Check the weather before setting out, but bear in mind that the actual weather, particularly in Scotland, can vary significantly from valley to valley and is often very different at the top from expectations at the bottom. For example, when I walked up Ben Macdui in the Cairngorms it was 20 degrees and very still in Aviemore, yet it was 10 degrees colder at the top and blowing a 50-mile-per-hour gale. Indeed I found it is pretty well always windier (usually much windier) at the very top compared to just below. A good rule of thumb is that the temperature falls about two degrees Celsius (excluding wind chill effects) with every thousand feet of height gained.

Meticulous **route planning** in advance pays off hugely. On many of the walks the routes are much better from certain start points than from others. Many of the routes and trip reports are available on the internet, but this can be pretty hit and miss as for some high points the information available (apart from the basic Ordnance Survey maps) is very thin or non-existent. One of the hardest, but also one of the most important, things to establish is the kind of terrain, particularly where footpaths do not exist, as it affects the severity and indeed feasibility of the route. Maps obviously help, but only provide part of the picture.

I found that **timing the route** in advance helped a lot, to ensure it would be feasible in the time available and also in setting expectations for others as to my return time. Naismith's rule is good for this – in my case I usually planned on 2.5 map miles per hour plus 1,250 feet of ascent per hour (plus a third of this for descent) plus time for stops plus/minus any adjustments for the type of terrain. Overall, I usually found the time going down took about the same as the time going up, as the speedier descent was usually offset by more time for stops. Going up, I found I made better progress if I stopped rarely and followed a 'slow and steady is best' principle.

Many people warned me in advance that **midges** would be a problem in Scotland. However, I hardly came across any. Apparently midges do not come out as much in sunshine or when it is windy or when it is cold (under 12 degrees or so). There are also fewer higher up in the hills.

Most people seem to assume that you will be able to phone for help if you have an incident in the mountains. This is not necessarily the case. My experience has been that **mobile phone** reception is usually non-existent or at best poor on most mountains.

I found I needed a few days' **recovery time** after a lengthy or tough day in the hills. I'm not sure why; it is presumably to do with age (I am 59 at the time of writing). The practical implication of this is that I could usually only tackle one or two high points on each trip, which is why I had to make as many as 50 trips on my *High Point* quest.

Finally, **three principles** stood me in good stead on my walks: have the right equipment (see kit list below), be prepared (so the worst does not happen, or can be minimised) and trust the map (it is always correct).

Kit for the walks
Pretty well all of my walks to the high points over 2,000 feet, and many others, were over rough, often remote country – so having proper kit was a must. This is what I took with me on each walk:

Clothing: The easiest way to stay comfortable when walking is to use a 'layering' system which you can adjust easily according to the conditions. Mine consisted of two base layer (not cotton) T-shirts with a high collar, one short-sleeved and one long-sleeved, a mid-layer fleece for warmth and a mid-layer windproof jacket when necessary. Walking trousers on my legs, with a scarf, sun protection hat and thin windproof gloves as needed. Over this I wore **weatherproof outer-wear:** a waterproof jacket and overtrousers, a warm storm hat and warm waterproof gloves.

Boots: I wore leather walking boots which lasted for my whole project and never gave me any trouble – highlighting the importance of proper fit. Whether you choose to buy leather or fabric boots (or walking shoes) is up to you, but ensure they fit well. I wore two pairs of socks, one thick and one thin to help avoid blisters.

On my back I had a **rucksack** (40 litre), to carry anything I was not wearing, plus a waterproof liner for the sack. Inside were:

A **first aid kit** containing small plasters, an ankle protector bandage, ibuprofen and a small Vaseline tin.

Food and water: Carry a sufficient quantity for your day, and consider emergency food. I carried lunch along with nuts, dried fruit, and two half-litre water bottles.

Sundry: survival bag (not used!). Whistle. Compass. Two copies of 1:25,000 and 1:50,000 map in a map case (to protect it against rain). Spare boot laces. Sun tan lotion. Spectacles. Sunglasses. Pen. Camera. Loo roll. Car keys. Plastic bags to protect camera, wallet and phone from the wet. Small torch. Wallet. Walking stick. Mobile phone. Phone numbers for emergencies.

If this seems like a lot of stuff, it is. I encountered several situations, particularly on the higher mountains, where at the start of the walk the weather was calm, dry and warm but at the top it was windy, wet and cold. I also visited many remote places, with no other people about for miles around – so proper survival kit is needed, even outside the winter months.

Also, **tell someone where you're going** so you can be found in extremis and leave a photocopy of your planned route with them. Easy to ignore, but I had an emergency when I broke my leg climbing Renfrewshire's Hill of Stake and this procedure was potentially life-saving.

Mountain Rescue

In case of an emergency dial **999** and ask for **Police** and then **Mountain Rescue**. Where possible give a six-figure grid reference of your location or that of the casualty. If you don't have reception where you are, try and attract the help of others around you. The usual distress signal is six short blasts on a whistle every minute. If you don't have a whistle, then shouting may work.

Mountain Rescue by SMS text

Another option in the UK is contacting the emergency services by SMS text – useful if you have a low battery or intermittent signal, but you do need to register your phone first. To register, simply text 'register' to 999 and then follow the instructions in the reply. Do it now – it could save yours or someone else's life. **www.emergencysms.org.uk**

The Countryside Code

Be safe – plan ahead

Even when going out locally, it's best to get the latest information about where and when you can go; for example, your rights to go onto some areas of open land may be restricted while work is carried out, for safety reasons or during breeding and shooting seasons. Follow advice and local signs, and be prepared for the unexpected.

- Refer to up-to-date maps or guidebooks.
- You're responsible for your own safety and for others in your care, so be prepared for changes in weather and other events.
- There are many organisations offering specific advice on equipment and safety, or contact visitor information centres and libraries for a list of outdoor recreation groups.
- Check weather forecasts before you leave, and don't be afraid to turn back.
- Part of the appeal of the countryside is that you can get away from it all. You may not see anyone for hours and there are many places without clear mobile phone signals, so let someone else know where you're going and when you expect to return.

Leave gates and property as you find them

Please respect the working life of the countryside, as our actions can affect people's livelihoods, our heritage, and the safety and welfare of animals and ourselves.

- A farmer will normally leave a gate closed to keep livestock in, but may sometimes leave it open so they can reach food and water. Leave gates as you find them or follow instructions on signs; if walking in a group, make sure the last person knows how to leave the gates.
- In fields where crops are growing, follow the paths wherever possible.
- Use gates and stiles wherever possible – climbing over walls, hedges and fences can damage them and increase the risk of farm animals escaping.
- Our heritage belongs to all of us – be careful not to disturb ruins and historic sites.
- Leave machinery and livestock alone – don't interfere with animals even if you think they're in distress. Try to alert the farmer instead.

Protect plants and animals, and take your litter home

We have a responsibility to protect our countryside now and for future generations, so make sure you don't harm animals, birds, plants or trees.

- Litter and leftover food doesn't just spoil the beauty of the countryside, it can be dangerous to wildlife and farm animals and can spread disease – so take your litter home with you. Dropping litter and dumping rubbish are criminal offences.
- Discover the beauty of the natural environment and take special care not to damage, destroy or remove features such as rocks, plants and trees. They provide homes and food

for wildlife, and add to everybody's enjoyment of the countryside.

- Wild animals and farm animals can behave unpredictably if you get too close, especially if they're with their young – so give them plenty of space.
- Fires can be as devastating to wildlife and habitats as they are to people and property – so be careful not to drop a match or smouldering cigarette at any time of the year. Sometimes, controlled fires are used to manage vegetation, particularly on heaths and moors between October and early April, so please check that a fire is not supervised before calling 999.

Keep dogs under close control

The countryside is a great place to exercise dogs, but it is the owner's duty to make sure their dog is not a danger or nuisance to farm animals, wildlife or other people.

- By law, you must control your dog so that it does not disturb or scare farm animals or wildlife. You must keep your dog on a short lead on most areas of open country and common land between 1 March and 31 July, and at all times near farm animals.
- You do not have to put your dog on a lead on public paths as long as it is under close control. But as a general rule, keep your dog on a lead if you cannot rely on its obedience. By law, farmers are entitled to destroy a dog that injures or worries their animals.
- If a farm animal chases you and your dog, it is safer to let your dog off the lead – don't risk getting hurt by trying to protect it.
- Take particular care that your dog doesn't scare sheep and lambs or wander where it might disturb birds that nest on the ground and other wildlife – eggs and young will soon die without protection from their parents.
- Everyone knows how unpleasant dog mess is and it can cause infections – so always clean up after your dog and get rid of the mess responsibly. Also make sure your dog is wormed regularly.

Consider other people

Showing consideration and respect for other people makes the countryside a pleasant environment for everyone – at home, at work and at leisure.

- Busy traffic on small country roads can be unpleasant and dangerous to local people, visitors and wildlife – so slow down and, where possible, leave your vehicle at home, consider sharing lifts and use alternatives such as public transport or cycling. For public transport information, phone Traveline on 0871 200 2233.
- Respect the needs of local people – for example, don't block gateways, driveways or other entry points with your vehicle.
- By law, cyclists must give way to walkers and horse riders on bridleways.
- Keep out of the way when farm animals are being gathered or moved and follow directions from the farmer.
- Support the rural economy – for example, buy your supplies from local shops.

How to use this book

This book is my personal account of walking to the highest point of each county in Great Britain. While it should provide a solid basis for your own high point journey, there is great scope to create your own personal quest by, for example, extending many of the walks or by starting from alternative points.

Each of the high points in this book is accompanied by additional information:

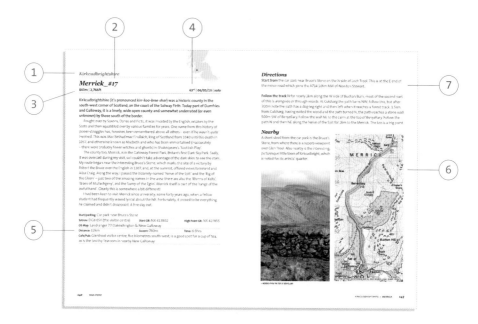

1. The county in which it features
2. Its ranking height relative to the other historic county high points
3. Its height in metres and feet
4. The order in which I made my ascent, the date and my companions (if any)

There is also an information panel **(5)** with details relating to my route to the high point: travel and parking, SATNAV and grid references, the relevant Ordnance Survey maps, distances and timings, and local cafes and pubs. An **Ordnance Survey 1:50,000 scale map** excerpt **(6)** and basic directions **(7)** provide information about my chosen routes to and from the tops. (Alternative routes are shown with a blue line on the maps.)

If you do intend to embark on your own high point quest, although this book should provide a good basis for your planning, I strongly recommend you undertake your own research into each high point and the best means of ascent. Consider the following points:

1. **Invest in and study the relevant maps** listed for each high point. Make sure you are able to read a map and use a compass, and are familiar with the symbols used on the maps. Bad weather or injury may precipitate an alternative route or shortcut.

2. Before setting out, **consider carefully your route**, the level of difficulty and the fitness/abilities of all members of your party. **If you are setting out on your own**, make sure someone knows when and where you are going and when you will be back.

▲ MORVEN, CAITHNESS

Maps, descriptions, distances, timings

While every effort has been made to maintain accuracy within the maps and descriptions in this book, we have had to process a vast amount of information and we are unable to guarantee that every single detail is correct.

Please exercise caution if a direction appears at odds with the route on the map. If in doubt, a comparison between the route, the description and a quick cross-reference with your map (along with a bit of common sense) should help ensure that you're on the right track. Note that distances have been measured off the map, and map distances rarely coincide 100% with distances on the ground. Please treat stated distances as a guideline only.

The time taken for the walks (as shown in the information panels in the gazetteer section) is calculated on a basis similar to Naismith's Rule and assumes: walking speed of 4 kilometres per hour, plus one hour per 400 metres gained, plus 15 minutes stoppage time per hour, plus extra time if the terrain is tricky – and rounded to the nearest half hour.

Ordnance Survey maps are the most commonly used, are easy to read and many people are happy using them. If you're not familiar with OS maps and are unsure of what the symbols mean, you can download a free OS 1:25,000 map legend from **www.ordnancesurvey.co.uk**

Here are a few of the symbols and abbreviations we use on the maps and in our directions:

 ROUTE STARTING POINT    ROUTE DIRECTION   HIGH POINT

GR = grid reference.

Km/mile conversion chart

Metric to Imperial

1 kilometre [km]	1000 m	0.6214 mile
1 metre [m]	100 cm	1.0936 yd
1 centimetre [cm]	10 mm	0.3937 in
1 millimetre [mm]		0.03937 in

Imperial to Metric

1 mile	1760 yd	1.6093 km
1 yard [yd]	3 ft	0.9144 m
1 foot [ft]	12 in	0.3048 m
1 inch [in]		2.54 cm

▲ LOCH LOMOND, SHIMMERING LIKE MERCURY, FROM BEN VORLICH

The Historic Counties

1. Aberdeenshire
2. Anglesey
3. Angus
4. Argyll
5. Ayrshire
6. Banffshire
7. Bedfordshire
8. Berkshire
9. Berwickshire
10. Brecknockshire
11. Buckinghamshire
12. Bute
13. Caernarfonshire
14. Caithness
15. Cambridgeshire
16. Cardiganshire
17. Carmarthenshire
18. Cheshire
19. Clackmannanshire
20. Cornwall
21. County Durham
22. Cumberland
23. Denbighshire
24. Derbyshire
25. Devon
26. Dorset
27. Dumfries-shire
28. Dunbartonshire
29. East Lothian
30. Essex
31. Fife
32. Flintshire
33. Glamorgan
34. Gloucestershire
35. Hampshire
36. Herefordshire
37. Hertfordshire
38. Huntingdonshire
39. Inverness-shire
40. Kent
41. Kincardineshire
42. Kinross-shire
43. Kirkcudbrightshire
44. Lanarkshire
45. Lancashire
46. Leicestershire
47. Lincolnshire
48. Merionethshire
49. Middlesex
50. Midlothian
51. Monmouthshire
52. Montgomeryshire
53. Morayshire
54. Nairnshire
55. Norfolk
56. Northamptonshire
57. Northumberland
58. Nottinghamshire
59. Orkney Islands
60. Oxfordshire
61. Peebles-shire
62. Pembrokeshire
63. Perthshire
64. Radnorshire
65. Renfrewshire
66. Ross and Cromarty
67. Roxburghshire
68. Rutland
69. Selkirkshire
70. Shetland Islands
71. Shropshire
72. Somerset
73. Staffordshire
74. Stirlingshire
75. Suffolk
76. Surrey
77. Sussex
78. Sutherland
79. Warwickshire
80. West Lothian
81. Western Isles
82. Westmorland
83. Wigtownshire
84. Wiltshire
85. Worcestershire
86. Yorkshire

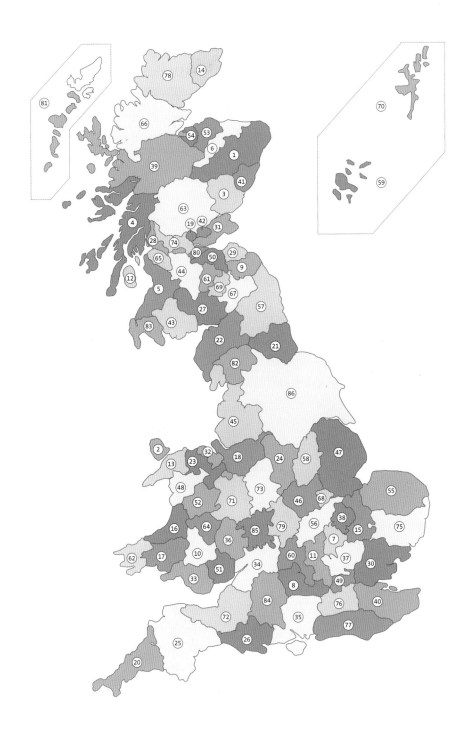

The year each county high point was climbed

Pre 2008	2008	2009

	Pre 2008	2008	2009
Counties:	5*	26**	25
Trips:	5	12	13

* Two of these were repeated (Westmorland in 2010, Worcestershire in 2011)

** Excl New Lancashire, New Yorkshire and Britain's Low Point

2010   **2011**   **2012**

Counties: *19****   *8*****   *3*

Trips: *12*   *6*   *3*

*** Excl Roxburghshire (Wikipedia definition)

**** Incl Western isles

County	High Point	Height
Inverness-shire	Ben Nevis	1,344m | 4,409ft
Aberdeenshire	Ben Macdui	1,309m | 4,295ft
Banffshire	Ben Macdui	1,309m | 4,295ft
Perthshire	Ben Lawers	1,214m | 3,983ft
Ross and Cromarty	Càrn Eige	1,183m | 3,881ft
Argyll	Bidean nam Bian	1,150m | 3,773ft
Caernarfonshire	Snowdon	1,085m | 3,560ft
Angus	Glas Maol	1,068m | 3,504ft
Sutherland	Ben More Assynt	998m | 3,274ft
Cumberland	Scafell Pike	978m | 3,209ft
Stirlingshire	Ben Lomond	974m | 3,196ft
Westmorland	Helvellyn	950m | 3,117ft
Dunbartonshire	Ben Vorlich	943m | 3,094ft
Merionethshire	Aran Fawddwy	905m | 2,969ft
Brecknockshire	Pen y Fan	886m | 2,907ft
Bute	Goatfell	874m | 2,867ft
Kirkcudbrightshire	Merrick	843m | 2,766ft
Peebles-shire	Broad Law	840m | 2,756ft
Selkirkshire	Broad Law	840m | 2,756ft
Denbighshire	Cadair Berwyn	827m | 2,713 ft
Montgomeryshire	Moel Sych	827m | 2,713ft
Dumfries-shire	White Coomb	821m | 2,694ft
Northumberland	The Cheviot	815m | 2,674ft
Lancashire (Old)	Old Man of Coniston	803m | 2,634ft
Western Isles	An Cliseam	799m | 2,621ft
Yorkshire (Old)	Mickle Fell	788m | 2,585ft
Carmarthenshire	Fan Foel	781m | 2,562ft
Kincardineshire	Mount Battock	778m | 2,552ft
Cardiganshire	Plynlimon	752m | 2,467ft
Lanarkshire	Cutler Fell	748m | 2,454ft
County Durham	Burnhope Seat	747m | 2,451ft
Roxburghshire	Hangingstone Hill	743m | 2,438ft
Yorkshire (New)	Whernside	736m | 2,415ft
Clackmannanshire	Ben Cleuch	721m | 2,365ft
Morayshire	Carn a Ghille Chearr	710m | 2,329ft
Caithness	Morven	706m | 2,316ft
Herefordshire	Black Mountain	703m | 2,306ft
Ayrshire	Blackcraig Hill	700m | 2,297ft
Monmouthshire	Chwarel y Fan	679m | 2,228ft
Radnorshire	Great Rhos	660m | 2,165ft
Nairnshire	Carn Glas-choire	659m | 2,162ft
Midlothian	Blackhope Scar	651m | 2,136ft
Derbyshire	Kinder Scout	636m | 2,087ft
Lancashire (New)	Gragareth	627m | 2,057ft

County	High Point	Height
Devon	High Willhays	621m | 2,037ft
Glamorgan	Craig y Llyn	600m | 1,969ft
West Lothian	West Cairn Hill	562m | 1,841ft
Cheshire	Shining Tor	559m | 1,834ft
Flintshire	Moel Famau	554m | 1,818ft
Shropshire	Brown Clee Hill	540m | 1,772ft
Pembrokeshire	Foel Cwmcerwyn	536m | 1,759ft
East Lothian	Meikle Says Law	535m | 1,755ft
Berwickshire	Meikle Says Law	535m | 1755ft
Fife	West Lomond	522m | 1,713ft
Renfrewshire	Hill of Stake	522m | 1,713ft
Staffordshire	Cheeks Hill	520m | 1,706ft
Somerset	Dunkery Beacon	519m | 1,703ft
Kinross-shire	Innerdouny Hill	497m | 1,631ft
Orkney Islands	Ward Hill	481m | 1,578ft
Shetland Islands	Ronas Hill	450m | 1,476ft
Worcestershire	Worcestershire Beacon	425m | 1,394ft
Cornwall	Brown Willy	420m | 1,378ft
Gloucestershire	Cleeve Cloud	330m | 1,083ft
Wigtownshire	Craig Airie Fell	322m | 1,056ft
Berkshire	Walbury Hill	297m | 974ft
Wiltshire	Milk Hill	295m | 968ft
Surrey	Leith Hill	295m | 968ft
Hampshire	Pilot Hill	286m | 919ft
Sussex	Black Down	280m | 919ft
Dorset	Lewesdon Hill	279m | 915ft
Leicestershire	Bardon Hill	278m | 912ft
Buckinghamshire	Haddington Hill	267m | 876ft
Warwickshire	Ebrington Hill	261m | 856ft
Oxfordshire	Whitehorse Hill	261m | 856ft
Kent	Betsom's Hill	251m | 823ft
Hertfordshire	Pavis Wood	244m | 801ft
Bedfordshire	Dunstable Downs	243m | 797ft
Northamptonshire	Arbury Hill	225m | 738ft
Anglesey	Holyhead Mountain	220m | 722ft
Nottinghamshire	Newtonwood Lane	205m | 673ft
Rutland	Cold Overton Park Wood	197m | 646ft
Lincolnshire	Normanby Top	168m | 551ft
Middlesex	Bushey Heath	155m | 509ft
Essex	Chrishall Common	147m | 482ft
Cambridgeshire	Great Chishill	146m | 479ft
Suffolk	Great Wood	128m | 420ft
Norfolk	Beacon Hill	105m | 344ft
Huntingdonshire	Boring Field	80m | 262ft
Britain's Low Point	Holme Fen	-3m | -9ft

Ben Macdui (Beinn Mac Duibh)_#2

1,309m | 4,295ft   Joint 45th | 25/06/09 | With Harry

Aberdeenshire is big, stretching from the east coast of Scotland into the centre of the country. On its coast sits Aberdeen, an ancient city often referred to as the 'oil capital of Europe'. Inland are the Highlands, a world away from the hustle and bustle of the city. Elsewhere, it's a little-known fact that much of Aberdeenshire is covered with lovely grassy fields which would seem at home in the south of England – fields often containing the famed Aberdeen Angus beef cattle native to both this county and the neighbouring Angus.

Aberdeenshire's county top is in the Cairngorm mountain range, home to some of the most dramatic scenery in Scotland, the only herd of reindeer in the country and one of the highest, snowiest and coldest areas in the UK – the Cairngorm Plateau.

The plateau is surrounded by five out of the six highest mountains in Britain. It's no surprise, then, that one of these, Ben Macdui, is the high point of the county, or that it is also the second highest peak in the UK. Covered in alpine tundra, it's a wonderfully desolate place in summer: barren, almost desert-like in places approaching the summit. In bad weather, it is a truly featureless navigational nightmare and it was good to have completed my walk in decent weather, as route-finding would have been tricky had thick cloud come down.

I had always been somewhat in awe of the scale, remoteness and potential difficulties of walking in the Cairngorms, so was pleased to finish my walk successfully. People often say you have to be careful of the weather here, and I can see what they mean – on our trip (with my son Harry, then aged eighteen) the weather was calm at the start but blowing a gale on top. Even though it was over 20 degrees Celsius in Aviemore, there were big patches of snow on the tops – in late June!

Start/parking: Cairngorm Mountain ski centre car park
Satnav: PH22 1RB   Start GR: NH 990060   High Point GR: NN 989989
OS Map: Landranger 36 Grantown and Aviemore; Landranger 43 Braemar & Blair Atholl
Distance: 17km   Ascent: 710m   Time: 8.5hrs
Café/Pub: The Ptarmigan Restaurant (01479 861336) at the top of the Cairngorm funicular railway claims to be the highest cafe in Britain. There is also the Cas Bar cafe at the ski centre Base Station.

Directions

Start from the ski centre car park, which is 15km SE of Aviemore and accessed by the B road which goes past Loch Morlich.

Follow the track SW then S for 4km, rising steadily to the spot point at 1083m. Follow the track 4km SSE across increasingly barren terrain, and with stunning views W to several munros across the valley, up to the summit of Ben Macdui. The top is a trig point, and is also the high point of Banffshire. The top can be very windy, even when the weather is calm at the ski centre!

Return the same way or, better still, after almost 2km retracing your steps, take the turn NNE for 2km to the 1111m spot point halfway between Cairn Lochan and Stob Coire an t-Sneachda. Then follow the top of the cliff face NE and then N for nearly 2km to the 1141m spot point; there are dramatic views SW from this route. Then take the track NW for 2km back to the ski centre.

Nearby

The Cairngorm Reindeer Centre. Reindeer were re-introduced into Scotland in 1952, and the herd has now grown to between 130 and 150 animals. The centre provides a good opportunity to encounter a herd living freely in their natural environment. Guided visits and treks take place every day, weather permitting. www.cairngormreindeer.co.uk

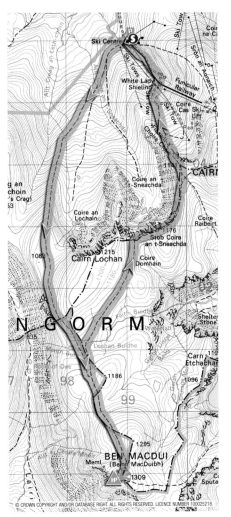

▲ HARRY HANGING ON IN STRONG WINDS ON TOP

Anglesey

Holyhead Mountain_#77

220m | 722ft   48th | 03/08/09 | with Alex and Annabel

Anglesey (or *Ynys Môn* in Welsh) is an island – the largest in Wales – sitting just off
the north-west corner of the country. The high point, Holyhead Mountain, lies on
Holy Island, which, in turn is the second largest island in Wales and sits just off the
west coast of the county.

About 75 per cent of Anglesey's inhabitants are Welsh speakers, a fact perhaps demon-
strated by the village of *Llanfairpwllgwyngyllgogerychwyrndrobwllllantysiliogogogoch* ('the
church of St Mary in a hollow of white hazel near a rapid whirlpool and near St Tysilio's
church by the red cave'). As you might guess, this is the longest place name in Britain,
dreamed up in the 19th century to attract tourists to the area.

Anglesey's entire rural coastline has been designated an Area of Outstanding Natural Beauty.
It was home of the noted Welsh painter Kyffin Williams, who stated in his autobiography
that during one year he observed some 90 separate bird species from his house overlooking
the Menai Straits. Impressive! Williams taught me art at school, sadly without much
success. I have his 'Pontllyfni in Snow' screenprint on my wall at home, which shows the
view towards Snowdon from Pontllyfni, just south of Caernarfon.

Holyhead Mountain sits right on the coast of Holy Island and overlooks South Stack
Lighthouse, a spectacular peninsula just to the north-west. On a clear day you can see Ireland
from its summit, and it's one of the first things you see on a ferry crossing from Dublin.
Perhaps surprisingly then, it is the lowest county high point in Wales. Notwithstanding
that, it has a surprisingly mountainous feel to it and is quite steep in parts towards the end.
I was joined by my wife Alex and her sister Annabel, a 'sister act'. We found our walk very
pleasant across pretty, heather moorland and met only a handful of people on our way.

Start/parking: Lakeside car park by Mountain Cottage

Satnav: LL65 1YF	**Start GR:** SH 226832	**High Point GR:** SH 218829
OS Map: Landranger 114 Anglesey		
Distance: 2.5km	**Ascent:** 200m	**Time:** 1.5hrs

Cafe/Pub: RSPB South Stack Cafe to the south of the mountain (01407 762100).

Directions

Start from the lakeside car park at Mountain Cottage, at the end of a minor road 3km W of Holyhead. This can be tricky to find; alternatively, park at Porth-y-felin on the minor road overlooking Holyhead harbour, and walk 1km NW, then SW towards the car park.

Follow the track past the N of the car park, WNW up towards North Stack. After 500m, and past the disused quarries, take the path SW. After 500m, at the crest of a rise, take the path SSE for 300m up to the top of Holyhead Mountain. The top is a trig point.

Nearby

20 kilometres ESE down the A55 is the interesting Oriel Kyffin Williams gallery at Llangefni. Sir Kyffin Williams, who died in 2006, was a local landscape painter and is considered one of the important Welsh artists of recent times. Nice cafe too. www.kyffinwilliams.info

▲ ANNABEL AND ALEX, THE 'SISTER ACT'

▲ LOOKING TOWARDS HOLYHEAD FROM HOLYHEAD MOUNTAIN

Glas Maol_#8

1,068m | 3,504ft   70ᵗʰ | 11/08/10 | solo

Like Aberdeenshire, the county of Angus stretches inland from Scotland's east coast towards the Highlands. The 10th-largest Scottish county, it was known as Forfarshire from the 18th century until 1928, a name taken from the county town of Forfar, at which point it reverted to Forfar. Angus' largest town, however, is Arbroath on the coast. Arbroath is a rather important town in the history of Scotland. It was here, in 1320, that the Declaration of Arbroath was made – a declaration that Scotland was an independent sovereign state and thus separate from England. Angus has since been touted as the 'birthplace' of Scotland.

At 1,068 metres, Glas Maol is not only the county top, but also the highest point in the Mounth range of hills, which, lying just south of the Cairngorms, form one of the more southerly parts of the Grampians. Glas Maol itself is quite near to Braemar and, with Balmoral nearby, the whole area has a 'royal' feel to it. Curiously, Glas Maol's big, flat summit actually lies within Aberdeenshire, Angus and Perthshire! (The actual high point is, however, in Angus.)

Sadly, my walk (the shortest route to the top) was spoiled a bit due to the presence of the Glenshee Ski Centre with its unsightly ski tows, fences and two of the largest car parks I have ever seen – both of which were empty on the day of my visit. I also experienced some of the Cairngorms' notorious windy weather and had to shorten my route. As I sat on the top of the mountain, I could see rain in the far distance but thought little of it – yet within moments was deluged!

Start/parking: Car park at the Glenshee Ski Centre on the A93

Satnav: PH10 7QF	**Start GR:** NO 139781	**High Point GR:** NO 167765

OS Map: Landranger 54 Dundee & Montrose

Distance: 6km	**Ascent:** 400m	**Time:** 3.5hrs

Cafe/Pub: Cafe by the car park at the Glenshee Ski Centre. Tasty dinner at the Gathering Place Bistro in nearby Braemar (01339 741234, www.the-gathering-place.co.uk).

▲ LOOKING DOWN GLEANN BEAG FROM MEALL ODHAR

Directions

Start from the car park at the Glenshee Ski Centre on the A93.

Follow the road S to the end of the huge car park. Take the track near the radio pylon NE and then, after 500m, ESE for 1km to the summit of Meall Odhar. The detritus of the ski facilities is left behind after this. Follow the track SE for 1km along to and up the steep side of Glas Maol and then 500m over the summit plateau to the top of Glas Maol. The top is a trig point.

An alternative and more appealing route, which I was unable to do because of poor (actually dreadful!) weather, begins in the in the car park 2.5km S of the ski centre, heads N along the Leacann Dubh ridge to Meall Odhar and E to the Glas Maol summit before returning S over Creag Leacach and W over Meall Gorm.

Nearby

Belonging to the Earls of Strathmore, Glamis Castle, set in a 14,000-acre estate, was the childhood home of the Queen Mother and the setting for Shakespeare's 'Macbeth'. Many myths surround the castle (monsters, ghosts and walled-up rooms) and events are organised through the year to reflect traditional Scottish culture and the Castle's history.
www.glamis-castle.co.uk

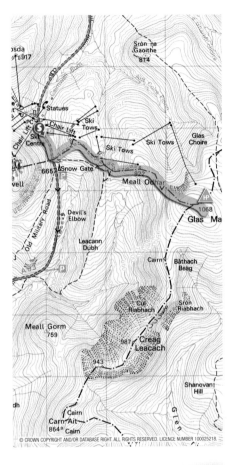

▲ GLAS MAOL SUMMIT

▲ LOOKING SOUTH-EAST FROM BIDEAN NAM BIAN TOWARDS STOB COIRE SGREAMHACH

Argyll

Bidean nam Bian_#6

1,150m | 3,773ft   83rd | 12/06/11 | solo

The lovely county of Argyll first came to my attention in the James Bond film *From Russia with Love* in the boat chase where 007 flees across the sea, leaving a trail of burning Spectre boats. In the film, this chase takes place on the Adriatic. In reality, it was shot on Loch Craignish, near Crinan. This is a beautiful part of the country, containing many of the islands that make up the Inner Hebrides – notably Mull, Islay and Jura (amongst others). Each of course has its own high point.

The historic county of Argyll no longer exists, replaced by Argyll and Bute. The two are broadly similar, with the modern county gaining ground to the south and west – but losing it to the north, where the historic high point lies. That high point is Bidean nam Bian in Glencoe. Glencoe is a stunning valley, famous for its dramatic mountainous scenery and for the Campbell clan's massacre of the MacDonalds in 1692. An interesting feature of my route is to walk along the unusual 'Lost Valley' where the MacDonalds are said to have hidden sheep rustled from Glencoe.

Hidden from the valley floor, Bidean nam Bian is a hulk of a mountain, referred to by some as the 'big beast'. Being the highest of the intimidating mountains which line both sides of Glencoe, it's easy to see why!

Choosing my route in advance was not easy as it was tricky to know the kind of terrain that would be encountered, so I went for the most straightforward option. I was glad I did, as the alternatives proved a bit exposed for comfort. The top itself was surprisingly calm for somewhere surrounded by such rocky cliffs, and the most difficult part of the walk was on the descent, at Bealach Dearg, where you have to negotiate a crevasse-like crack which seems impossible from above. Having seen a couple successfully tackle this obstacle, I followed and – luckily – found it to be easier than it appeared.

Start/parking: Car park on A82

Satnav: GLENCOE	**Start GR:** NN 170569	**High Point GR:** NN 143542
OS Map: Landranger 41 Ben Nevis		
Distance: 9km	**Ascent:** 1,050m	**Time:** 7 hours

Cafe/Pub: Nice tea and cakes at the Crafts & Things Coffee Shop (01855 811325, www.craftsandthings.co.uk), just off the A82 between Ballachulish and Glencoe village. Superb seafood dinner at the Lochleven Seafood Cafe, on the B863 halfway along the north bank of Loch Leven (01855 821048, www.lochlevenseafoodcafe.co.uk).

Directions

Start from the car park on the S side of the A82, approximately 8km E of Glencoe village, marked on the map as a viewpoint and helipad.

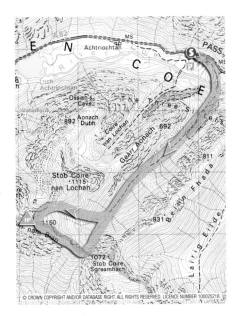

Head SE for 500m along a bridleway and then footpath to a footbridge over the River Coe. Cross the river and then follow the path SW uphill along the W side of (and above) the Allt Coire Gabhail stream which is below. This path goes for approximately 1km along the N side, and then through woods; towards the end of this stretch the path crosses some stone slabs which would be a little tricky to negotiate in the wet. At the end of the woods the path levels out and you enter the 'Lost Valley'.

© CROWN COPYRIGHT AND/OR DATABASE RIGHT. ALL RIGHTS RESERVED. LICENCE NUMBER 100025218.

Follow the path SW along the valley for 1.5km, at which point the path diverges. (The path straight ahead up towards Bealach Dearg at 944m is the route you will return down later.) Take the path W for 1km along a stream and then WNW up to the bealach at 1,000m between Bidean nam Bian and Stob Coire nan Lochan; this path rises steeply over grassy ground and becomes indistinct after a while. Follow the crest of the ridge steeply upwards SW over rocky ground for 300m up to the summit of Bidean nam Bian. The summit is a cairn.

To return, take the ridge ESE for 1km down to Bealach Dearg. Then head NE down to the Lost Valley; this is very steep, and quite tricky, initially and then goes down scree. An alternative return option is to go NE from Bidean nam Bian to the 1,115m Stob Coire nan Lochan, and then down to Coire nan Lochan and the start point.

Nearby

The scenery in and around Glencoe is breathtaking. The Glencoe Visitor Centre (www.glencoe-nts.org.uk) is a good place to find out more about it. The more active could try indoor ice-climbing at Kinlochleven (www.ice-factor.co.uk) or drive north to Fort William and tackle Ben Nevis, the highest of all the high points (p134)!

▲ LOOKING TOWARDS LOCH ETIVE FROM BIDEAN NAM BIAN

Blackcraig Hill_#37

700m | 2,297ft

64th | 07/05/10 | solo

Ayrshire lies in south-west Scotland, between Glasgow and the coast, and has a long coastline that hugs the Firth of Clyde. It is one of the more fertile regions of Scotland – helped in part to by the people of Ayrshire exploiting their proximity to the sea and using a seaweed-based fertiliser to feed their crops. As a result, the area is known for its agriculture, with strawberries and potatoes grown in large quantities. The county is also renowned for the high quality of its bacon!

Sports fans might also recognise the county as being home to the famous Troon and Turnberry golf courses, which have hosted the Open Championship eight and four times respectively. They might also know that the Open was, in fact, created in Ayrshire, at Prestwick Golf Club in 1860. Football fans may know that the county was the birthplace of Liverpool legend Bill Shankly.

The county top is Blackcraig Hill, which lies in a particularly beautiful part of the county about 20 kilometres south-east of Ayr and just north of Galloway. Sandwiched between the Lowther Hills and Galloway Forest Park, it is an area full of rolling hills and thick forests. I was in two minds about doing the walk, as I had mildly sprained my ankle the day before on the Merrick, but the terrain was straightforward (grassy heathland slopes) so I went ahead anyway – and all turned out well. It was a quiet day, and I met no one on my walk.

Start/parking: On minor road from New Cumnock

Satnav: NEW CUMNOCK   **Start GR:** NS 631080   **High Point GR:** NS 647064

OS Map: Landranger 71 Lanark & Upper Nithsdale; Landranger 77 Dalmellington & New Galloway

Distance: 8km   **Ascent:** 430m   **Time:** 4hrs

Cafe/Pub: Nardini's, Largs (see 'Nearby', 01475 675000, www.nardinis.co.uk).

▲ BLACKCRAIG HILL SUMMIT PLATEAU

Directions

Start just after the turn to Blackcraig farm, on the E verge of the minor road which goes S from New Cumnock towards Afton Reservoir. This spot is 5km S of New Cumnock, and 2km N of the car park by the Afton Filter Station further down the road.

Follow the track ENE towards Blackcraig farm. Continue past the farm for 2km, E then SE up to Quintin Knowe; this is the intersection point between the track and a fence. Follow the fence SSW for 1.5km up Blackcraig Hill; the path is indistinct along this stretch, and goes steadily upwards over grassy slopes before levelling off. The top is a trig point.

Nearby

It's a bit of a drive, but why not make the trip west to the town of Largs – a pleasant coastal town and home to the famous Nardini's restaurant and ice cream parlour, 2006 and 2008 UK Ice Cream Champion of Champions! www.nardinis.co.uk

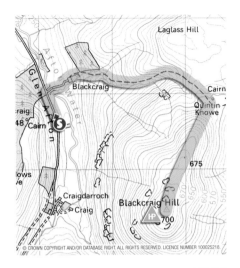

▲ BLACKCRAIG HILL SUMMIT

▲ BLACKCRAIG HILL SUMMIT PLATEAU

Ben Macdui (Beinn Mac Duibh)_#2

1,309m | 4,295ft   Joint 45th | 25/06/09 | with Harry

The County of Banff, also known as Banffshire, no longer exists and its lands are now split between Moray and Aberdeenshire. It was, at any rate, something of a 'messy' county: until 1891 it contained several exclaves – areas of land controlled by the county, but entirely separate from it and situated inside Aberdeenshire, some many miles from the rest of the county.

    This historic county runs along the south side of the Moray Firth and then inland to the Cairngorm Mountains – which is where you'll find the high point, Ben Macdui. If you have already climbed the county top of Aberdeenshire, you will already have been up Ben Macdui – in which case you have earned yourself two ticks, as the peak is on the border of the two counties, making it the highest point in both. See the Aberdeenshire entry on page 46 for more information on the peak.

    Whilst it was the county town of Banff that gave its name to the county, and it is Buckie, on the coast, which is the largest, it is the town of Portsoy which is perhaps the most interesting. With a charming, character-filled old town and harbour which date back some 300 years, Portsoy is famous for its green 'marble' (actually serpentine, not marble), which was frequently made into jewellery and some of which was considered fine enough to find its way into the fixtures and fittings in the grand Palace of Versailles in France. Less famously, but significant in a family context, my wife's great great grandfather was, in the 1860s, the local policeman in Portsoy.

    Skiing aficionados will be familiar with another Banff – the Canadian resort town in Alberta. This town, and later its national park, was named in 1884 by George Stephen, the president of the Canadian Pacific Railway, in honour of his birthplace in Banffshire.

Start/parking: Cairngorm Mountain ski centre car park

Satnav: PH22 1RB	**Start GR:** NH 990060	**High Point GR:** NN 989989

OS Map: Landranger 36 Grantown and Aviemore; Landranger 43 Braemar & Blair Atholl

Distance: 17km	**Ascent:** 710m	**Time:** 8.5hrs

Café/Pub: The Ptarmigan Restaurant (01479 861336) at the top of the Cairngorm funicular railway claims to be the highest cafe in Britain. There is also the Cas Bar cafe at the ski centre Base Station.

Full details of the walk can be found on p46 for Aberdeenshire.

Nearby

Visit the Ruthven Barracks, a few miles south near Kingussie. There have been castles and forts on this site since the 1200s and the remains of an imposing 18th-century castle can still be visited. A strategically important site, it was here that Alexander Stewart, the 'Wolf of Badenoch', died and it was here that the Jacobean Uprising came to a symbolic end when the Jacobites learned that their leader, Bonny Prince Charlie, was in flight.

▲ BEN MACDUI SUMMIT

▲ BEN MACDUI SUMMIT PLATEAU

Dunstable Downs_#75

243m | 797ft   39th | 22/04/09 | solo

Bedfordshire is sometimes thought to be a quite nondescript county – perhaps overlooked due to its proximity to London or its lack of any striking natural features. Look closer, however, and this seems a little unfair – Bedfordshire contains the Luton Hoo country house, a magnificent building dating back to the 18th century; Whipsnade Zoo, which is the UK's biggest zoo; and Woburn Abbey, home to one of the finest private art collections in the world. And we shouldn't forget the lovely Chiltern Hills, a heavily wooded Area of Outstanding Natural Beauty which stretch into the southern end of the county.

Bedfordshire also contains the lovely Dunstable Downs – the county top – about 20 kilometres south-west of Luton, near Whipsnade Zoo. A grassy area of chalk escarpment, they offer fantastic and wide-ranging views over the county. Much of the top is open grassland, which makes them popular with hang gliders, paragliders and kite flyers, as well as families on picnic trips and the like – there were many people on the downs the day I was there, but none at the trig point, which I would guess is rarely visited. I found the top bizarrely difficult to find, even though it is right by the entrance to the Dunstable Downs Visitor Centre.

I completed my walk after having heard the Chancellor Alistair Darling deliver the Budget, and George Osborne give his reply to it, on the drive up from London.

Start/parking: Car park at Dunstable Downs visitor centre

Satnav: LU6 2TA	**Start GR:** TL 008194	**High Point GR:** TL 008194
OS Map: Landranger 166 Luton & Hertford		
Distance: 0.5km	**Ascent:** 0m	**Time:** 0.5hrs

Cafe/Pub: Cafe in the Dunstable Downs Countryside Centre, right next to the high point.

Directions

Start from the car park at the Dunstable Downs visitor centre. This is on the B4541 just S of Dunstable.

Walk to the entrance of the car park. The top is a trig point, just S of the entrance.

Nearby

The UK's biggest zoo, Whipsnade is home to almost 3,000 animals in an impressive 600-acre site. There are daily events including animal shows and talks, and visitors can drive their own cars through an 'Asia Experience' area. The zoo is open every day of the year, bar Christmas Day. www.zsl.org/whipsnade

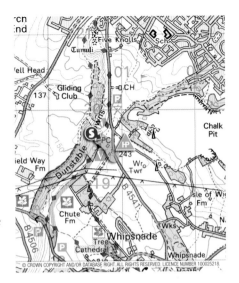

▲ LOOKING NORTH-WEST FROM DUNSTABLE DOWNS

Berkshire

Walbury Hill_#63

297m | 974ft

8th | 20/06/08 | solo

Berkshire is one of the oldest counties in England. It appears to have first been recorded in the ninth century, with the monk and writer Asser noting that the county took its name from a large forest known as *Bearroc* (which meant 'hilly' in Celtic). The county boundaries have remained relatively static since that time, stretching slightly over the years to include Slough in the east and Didcot and Wantage in the west.

 Berkshire is possibly most noted for containing Windsor Castle, Ascot, Newbury and Windsor racecourses and the M4 motorway. Perhaps less well-known is that Berkshire contains Highclere Castle (of *Downton Abbey* fame), the Royal Military Academy at Sandhurst and is where the Prime Minister David Cameron was brought up and went to school (at Eton).

 The county highpoint is Walbury Hill, which, at 297 metres, is not only the highest natural point in Berkshire, but also, some say, in South East England – sitting just three metres higher than Leith Hill in Surrey. However, as Walbury Hill lies to the west of Newbury, it could be argued that it's not really in the South East ... Regardless, the hill is situated in the pretty, but not generally well known, North Wessex Downs Area of Outstanding Natural Beauty, a lovely part of the country marked by open downland and chalk hills. It is actually part of the same chalk formation which runs across southern England and culminates in the South Downs. The summit of Walbury Hill is marked by the Iron Age hill fort of Walbury Camp – the largest hill fort in Berkshire and one of a significant number of similar sites in the region. The true high point is, however, 100 metres further south and is marked by a trig point. The hill is also occasionally, thanks to its prominence, used by the BBC as a temporary relay station during major sporting events.

Start/parking: Car park on east side of Walbury Hill

Satnav: UPPER GREEN (Nearest)   **Start GR:** SU 378616   **High Point GR:** SU 373616

OS Map: Landranger 174 Newbury & Wantage

Distance: 2km   **Ascent:** 40m   **Time:** 1hr

Cafe/Pub: Nice coffee and cakes at the Azuza Coffee Shop in nearby Hungerford (01488 644643).

Directions

Start from the car park on the E side of Walbury Hill. This is on a road 3km SSE from Inkpen to Faccombe.

Follow the Wayfarer's Walk track WNW for 500m. Go SSW through a gate for 300m along a path to Walbury Hill. The top is a trig point, in the middle of a big field, and is not visible from the track.

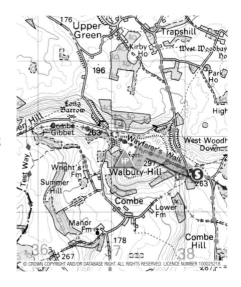

Nearby

Extend your walk two kilometres southeast and visit Pilot Hill – the county top of Hampshire (p126). Alternatively, Highclere Castle is only a short distance away. The castle famously features in the television series *Downton Abbey* and was once home to the fifth Earl of Carnarvon – locater of Tutankhamun's tomb. An Egyptian exhibition celebrates his discovery. www.highclerecastle.co.uk

▲ WALBURY HILL SUMMIT

Berwickshire

Meikle Says Law_#50

535m | 1755ft   Joint 57th | 22/10/09 | with Alex

Berwickshire is a Scottish county that takes its name from an English town. That town being the market town of Berwick-upon-Tweed, which sits in the lovely Scottish Borders area, right on the line between the two countries, and which has changed hands more than once. Originally part of the 'Kingdom of England', it came under Scottish control around 1000 AD and soon gave the county its name. It was then ceded to the English, sold back to the Scots and then swapped back and forth until, nearly 500 years later during the Anglo-Scottish wars, the town was taken by the English, becoming part of the county of Northumberland, where it has remained ever since, leaving Berwickshire without its namesake. The county has since occasionally been known as Dunsshire, after Duns, the new county town.

Travelling north across the county, away from England and to the opposite county border, you'll find the county high point, Meikle Says Law. An extensive grouse moor in the Lammer-muir Hills, with heather all around, it sits on the border with the county of East Lothian and is the high point of both counties. The Lammermuir Hills, despite being a relatively low-lying range, are a fairly imposing set of hills. They are crossed by only one road and have a notable lack of passes through them, meaning that they create a natural barrier between the Scottish Borders and Edinburgh. That said, my walk up turned out to be quite straightforward. Alex and I met no one on the walk, but as we returned to our car a fleet of half a dozen Land Rovers arrived, each full of men with guns – there for the grouse shooting. Their arrival with guns, in such a remote and beautiful spot, was quite alarming!

Start/parking: Road verge
Satnav: GIFFORD (nearest)   **Start GR:** NT 612636   **High Point GR:** NT 581617
OS Map: Landranger 67 Duns, Dunbar & Eyemouth
Distance: 8km   **Ascent:** 190m   **Time:** 3.5hrs
Cafe/Pub: Try The Victoria Inn, Haddington (01620 823332).

Directions

Start from the north verge of the minor road 500m NE of Faseny Cottage and 1.5km SE from the B6355.

Follow the track down and past Faseny Cottage. Cross Faseny Water and follow the track W along the N side of Lamb Burn. The track winds SW, then NW, then W (past Dun Side) and finally SW (past Sheil Rig) until it reaches Meikle Says Law. In the early stretch, the track crosses burns half a dozen or so times. The track goes steadily upwards through grouse moor. The top is a trig point, and is also the high point of East Lothian (p114).

Nearby

Why not travel south to Melrose Abbey, home and possible burial place of Robert the Bruce?

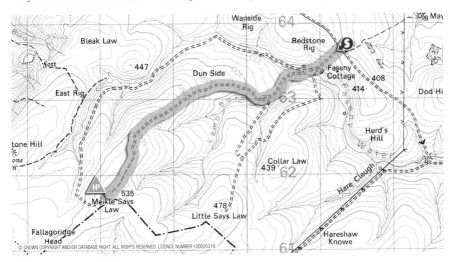

▲ ON TOP OF MEIKLE SAYS LAW, LOOKING OUT OVER THE LAMMERMUIR HILLS

Brecknockshire

Pen y Fan_#15

886m | 2,907ft   17th | 07/08/08 | with Harry

The county top of Brecknockshire is Pen y Fan. At 886 metres, it is not only the highest point in the county, but also the highest point in the Brecon Beacons National Park and the highest point in the UK south of Snowdonia. A striking mountain, with scalloped and scooped sides of bare, grassy moorland, it towers over the surrounding countryside. Its peak, a twin summit formed with the slightly lower Corn Du (873m), was formerly referred to as 'Arthur's Seat' and offers marvellous views – a patchwork quilt of fields on one side, and the rougher, wilder Brecon Beacons on the other.

The Brecon Beacons National Park was established in 1957, becoming the third national park in Wales at the time. Stretching for almost 50 miles across south Wales, it encompasses several distinct regions – the Brecon Beacons themselves, the Black Mountains and Fforest Fawr (the Great Forest). It is unsurprising, then, that the park contains a striking variety of landscapes, from high moorland and scooped hillsides to farmed valleys, thick forests and spectacular waterfalls.

An immensely popular peak to visit, Pen y Fan notoriously features in the fitness and navigational selection processes of the UK Special Forces (i.e. the SAS and SBS), as part of a 24-kilometre long 'Fan Dance' exercise. My visit was perhaps a little easier – the walk is a lovely horseshoe route and straightforward to navigate, although the day is quite a long one. It was very nice to complete this walk with Harry, who was 18 at the time. We came across about 20 people during the day.

Start/parking: Car park west of Talybont Reservoir.

Satnav: ABER (nearest)	**Start GR:** SO 055175	**High Point GR:** SO 012215
OS Map: Landranger 160 Breacon Beacons		
Distance: 16km	**Ascent:** 700m	**Time:** 7hrs

Cafe/Pub: Two kilometres south along the road, just before the Pentwyn Reservoir, there is a nice cafe at Ystradgynwyn – The Old Barn Tea Room (01685 383358).

Nearby

The interesting 'book town' of Hay-on-Wye is a short distance away. There are well over two dozen bookshops in this pretty little town, with many offering specialist and second-hand titles. www.hay-on-wye.co.uk

▲ PEN Y FAN SUMMIT

Directions

Start from the car park at the intersection of the Taff Trail and the Beacons Way, 4km W of the Talybont Reservoir.

Follow the path NNW along the side of the wood and then N up to Craig y Fan Ddu.

Continue 2km NW and N, and then NE along Graig Fan Las, until the path meets another path 300m NE of the 754m spot point. Head SW and then NW for 3km along Bwlch y Ddwyallt, Craig Cwareli and Craig Cwmoergwm until reaching the top of Fan y Big. Continue along the ridge W and then NW up to Cribyn, and onwards W down and then up to Pen y Fan. The top is a cairn.

Return via the other side of the valley. Go WSW to Corn Du and then SSW for 400m down to Bwlch Duwynt. Then go SE along the ridge for 2.5km until you reach a cairn where the path diverges. Turn ESE and go down sharply and then over grassy slopes for 1.5km down to the Filter House below the Upper Neuadd Reservoir. Take the track for 2km SSE and then SE and E through the Taf Fechan Forest. Then turn NE and go along the road for 1km back to the car park.

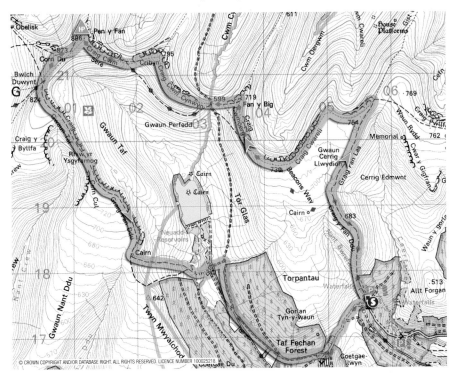

▲ THE VIEW FROM BWLCH DUWYNT TO PEN Y FAN AND CRIBYN

Haddington Hill_#70

267m | 876ft   11th | 26/06/08 | solo

Buckinghamshire sits right in the middle of southern England, bordering seven other historic counties. It is one of the Home Counties and one of the wealthiest in the country, with apparently the highest GDP per head of anywhere outside London. The southern boundary of the county (with Berkshire) is marked by the River Thames, which flows from Gloucestershire into the City, although the county as a whole is a little too far from London to be considered prime commuter territory.

There's a marked divide in the landscape of Buckinghamshire. In the north, it's relatively flat and agricultural, while the south contains the lovely Chiltern Hills. These are a heavily-wooded range of hills, designated an Area of Outstanding Natural Beauty, which stretch across four counties, from Oxfordshire to Hertfordshire. Haddington Hill, Buckinghamshire's county top, is also the highest point in the Chilterns and is one of those high points which you barely have to step out of your car to visit. Situated in Wendover Woods, you can park in the middle of the woods and then, just five minutes or so later, be sitting on a bench just by the high point, which is marked by a stone. It is a somewhat bizarre county top: a high point without a view, a cul-de-sac in a small clearing in the woods at the end of a short path, a route so easy you could walk to it in slippers. No one else was there.

Start/parking: Wendover Woods car park

Satnav: HP22 5NQ	**Start GR:** SP 888090	**High Point GR:** SP 890089
OS Map: Landranger 165 Aylesbury & Leighton Buzzard		
Distance: 0.5km	**Ascent:** 0m	**Time:** 0.5hrs

Cafe/Pub: Wendover Woods Cafe, (www.forestry.gov.uk/wendoverwoods), or have a BBQ on the free BBQ stands!

Directions

Start from the Wendover Woods car park, approximately 2km SE of Halton. The entrance to the car park is 1km up a minor road which can be accessed from the B4009 S of Aston Clinton and ENE of Halton.

Follow the track S then E for 300m to the summit of Haddington Hill. The top is a standing stone, surrounded by trees.

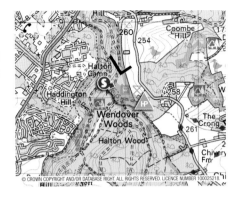

Nearby

Buckinghamshire has many places of interest including the Cliveden and Waddesdon Manor historic houses, the Ashridge Estate, Enigma code-breaking Bletchley Park, the delightful Bekonscot model village, and Dorney rowing lake – which was used in the 2012 Olympics.

▲ THE TOP OF HADDINGTON HILL

Bute

Goatfell (Gaoda Bheinn)_ #16

874m | 2867ft

86th | 14/08/11 | solo

Seemingly more sea than land, the historic County of Bute comprises several small islands in the Firth of Clyde, just south-west of Glasgow. Principal among these are Bute and Arran; the former containing Rothesay, the county town, and the latter the high point, Goatfell.

Arran is often described as 'Scotland in miniature' as it has its own 'highlands' and 'lowlands'. As on the mainland, these are created by the Highland Boundary Fault – a major geographical feature which separates the two areas of distinct geology. The nickname is a fair description in other ways too: Arran seems to capture the essence of Scotland through lovely features such as the mountains down the centre of the island, the little villages around the coast and the lovely Brodick Castle gardens (and also less lovely features, like Brodick itself – a touristy place of little charm).

At 874 metres, Goatfell is one of four Corbetts (peaks between 2,500 and 3,000 feet) on Arran. With a relatively accessible nature and views stretching to Ireland, it's a popular peak and can be busy. Half an hour after I reached the top, it became overrun and noisy, so I quickly moved on.

My route up Goatfell was the on-the-face-of-it uninspiring 'tourist route' from Brodick – I chose this both for convenience and so as not to overdo it, as I was planning another walk (Renfrewshire's later-to-be-dreaded Hill of Stake) a couple of days later. I started well before the tourist ferry from Ardrossan had arrived and so had the path to myself. The views across the sea were lovely, but the walk became most memorable when I reached the top and saw for the first time the superb, unexpected vista of the mountains to the north-west. This was one of the very best views from any of the high points I visited and a delightful surprise.

It was in Arran that my high point exploits first gained wider attention, when the local newspaper, the *Arran Banner*, published an article about me after my visit!

Start/parking: Car park on the A841 opposite The Wineport cafe

Satnav: KA27 8DE   **Start GR:** NS 012375   **High Point GR:** NR 991415

OS Map: Landranger 69 Isle of Arran

Distance: 9.5km   **Ascent:** 870m   **Time:** 6.5hrs

Cafe/Pub: Nice tea spot at the Wineport bistro/cafe, with its suntrap terrace, at the start of the walk (01770 302101, www.wineport.co.uk).

Directions

Start from the car park on the A841 approximately 2km N of the ferry terminal at Brodick. This car park is just across the road from the complex which includes the Wineport cafe, Arran Brewery and Cladach Pottery.

Cross the road and go to the courtyard behind the Wineport cafe, then go past the Arran Brewery shop until the courtyard becomes a bridleway in the far left corner of the courtyard. Follow the bridleway, which winds W and then NW through the woods. Some paths join and leave the route and after 500m the route crosses the road to Brodick Castle. All the while follow the signposts NNW to Goatfell, and after approximately 1.5km you will be clear of the woods and onto moorland. The path from here is straightforward and well trodden. Initially it goes NNW above the E side of Cnocan Burn, then N up to the cairn on the ridge between Goatfell and Meall Breac. It is approximately 5km from the start to this point. Then follow the path W and steeply up for 600m to the summit of Goatfell. The top is a trig point, with superb views, particularly to the dramatic mountains to the NW.

Return by retracing your steps, or alternatively via Glen Rosa. To do this, head N from Goatfell to North Goatfell and then NW to The Saddle. Then take the footpath S down the Glen Rosa valley and back to Brodick.

Nearby

Brodick Castle and Gardens are virtually underneath Goatfell. The castle was home to the Duke and Duchess of Montrose, and is virtually unchanged since then, with most of the original furnishings still in place. The Gardens, meanwhile, are set in beautiful woodlands and contain a fairytale-like Bavarian summerhouse. (0844 493 2152)

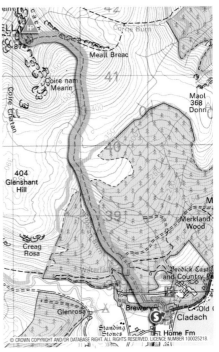

▲ GOATFELL SUMMIT LOOKING NORTH-WEST

▲ LOOKING NORTH FROM GOATFELL TOWARDS NORTH GOATFELL AND THE SOUND OF BUTE

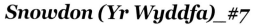

Caernarfonshire

Snowdon (Yr Wyddfa)_#7

1,085m | 3,560ft   1st | Sept. 2003* | with Harry

*Also climbed several times in the late 1960s and early 1970s with Highgate School

Caernarfonshire stretches across the north-west tip of Wales, starting at the sea and heading inland to the mountains. Bordered by the Irish Sea and the Menai Strait, the top of the county is relatively flat, home to the seaside town of Llandudno, and to the Llŷn Peninsula. Move south, and the land rears up into Snowdonia National Park. The first national park in Wales and the third in the UK, Snowdonia, *Eryri* in Welsh, is a wild and dramatic place, full of myths and legends. Its steep-sided valleys are dark and circled by jagged crags and imposing peaks, while reminders of the slate-mining industry are ever-present in slag heaps and abandoned quarries.

Snowdon itself is, at 3,560 feet, the highest mountain in England and Wales. Notorious for having a cafe on its summit (described by Prince Charles as 'the highest slum in Wales'), it is a popular peak. The first recorded rock climb in Britain took place on Snowdon in 1798 and Edmund Hillary's 1953 Everest expedition trained on its slopes. Less energetic visitors can take a train – the Snowdon Mountain Railway – from Llanberis right to the top of the mountain!

My ascent of Snowdon felt familiar – I had climbed it several times as a teenager on Duke of Edinburgh's Award school trips. I was, however, particularly excited as I was accompanied by Harry, who was only 13 and Snowdon was his first 'high' mountain (1,000 feet or so higher than those he had climbed before in the Yorkshire Dales). The weather was wet throughout our ascent, so all credit to Harry for sticking so resolutely to the task. We took the Pyg Track up and the Miners' Track down, but the experience was somewhat spoiled as there were probably about 1,000 or so people on the mountain that day (a Saturday in September). Next time, I will take the less popular Rhyd-Ddu path. I recall we had a lovely venison steak for dinner, which I think to an extent accounts for Harry being keen on venison to this day.

Start/parking: Pen-y-Pass car park
Satnav: LL55 4NU   Start GR: SH 647556   High Point GR: SH 610543
OS Map: Landranger 115 Snowdon/Yr Wyddfa
Distance: 9.5km   Ascent: 730m   Time: 6.5hrs
Cafe/Pub: Cafe at Pen-y-Pass. You can also get a nice beer at the nearby Pen-y-Gwryd Hotel, about 1.5 kilometres east. (01286 870211, www.pyg.co.uk).

Directions

Start from the Pen-y-Pass car park opposite the Gorphwysfa cafe. This is on the A4086, 1.5km W of the Pen-y-Gwryd hotel. Aim to be at the start before 9 a.m. or the car park may well be full – the Snowdon climb is very popular, particularly at weekends!

Follow the track WSW for 1.3km to Bwlch y Moch. This becomes quite steep and then levels off just before Llyn Llydaw becomes visible. Take the Pyg Track SW then W for 2.5km; this rises steadily and then sharply until it reaches the railway line at Bwlch Glas.

(**An alternative from Bwlch y Moch** for the adventurous is to take the steep path up Crib Goch and then scramble along the very exposed ridge to Crib y Ddysgl and along to Bwlch Glas – experienced mountain walkers only!)

Head SSE from Bwlch Glas for 500m, up along the railway line to the Snowdon summit. There is a cafe, usually very busy, on top. The top is a (busy!) trig point.

Return to Bwlch Glas and set off back down the Pyg Track. After 500m the path splits; take the right branch steeply down the Miners' Track down to Glaslyn. Continue the Miners Track along and then across Llyn Llydaw back down to Pen-y-Pass.

An alternative route down from the Snowdon summit is to go south-east down the steep scree to the col, and then up Y Lliwedd. Then follow the cliff face for 700m round NE until the path leads north for 1km down to the Miners' Track at the Llyn Llydaw causeway.

For a longer, more adventurous walk, try the full Snowdon Horseshoe, including both Crib Goch and Y Lliwedd. When I was a teenager at school, I managed to complete the whole horseshoe in just four hours eight minutes!

Nearby
Visit the Electric Mountain in Llanberis. Elidir Mountain, above the lake, is hollow, hiding a huge hydro-electric power station – one of the largest in Europe – with huge underground chambers and tunnels big enough to swallow a bus. www.electricmountain.co.uk

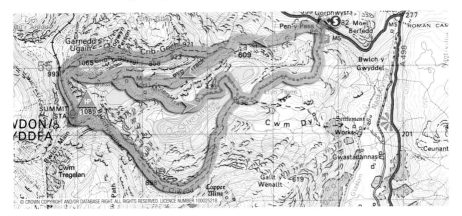

Morven_#35

706m | 2,316ft   80th | 10/05/11 | solo

You cannot get further north on the British mainland than Caithness. Lying right on the north-east tip of Scotland, the county is best known for the town of John o'Groats – start of the 874-mile traverse of Britain to Land's End in Cornwall. The town isn't the most northerly point though – that honour lies with Easter Head, about 18 kilometres further west.

Caithness is a little-known county and much of it is the remote, barren Flow Country, which is a real wilderness and Europe's largest expanse of blanket peat bog. Caithness is, however, a treat to visit, full of interesting spots including the Forsinard nature reserve (in the middle of the Flow Country), Kildonan (the scene of a gold rush in 1869), the Castle of Mey (where the Queen Mother lived for many years), Lybster harbour (which was in the 19th century the third-largest herring fishing port in Scotland, after Wick and Fraserburgh, with over 300 boats), and the two long Grey Cairns of Camster (built over 5,000 years ago). I was nervous about climbing Morven as it is a very conical, boulder-strewn mountain and I knew from my previous research that the route was little-walked, hard to find and remote. All of this turned out to be true and indeed I saw no one all day. Furthermore, the approach walk is past the somewhat intimidating and impossibly-steep-seeming Maiden Pap. Even the start of the route felt a bit nerve-wracking, as deer culling (with rifles) takes place at certain times of the year, which gave me some unease even though I knew it was out of season. Then, when I got to the top, the wind was so strong that I could hardly stand up. All in all, I was glad to get back safely!

Note: Deer culling takes place between August and January. It is advisable to confirm the feasibility of access with the Welbeck Estate (01593 751237) before travelling.

Start/parking: Phone box 500m W of Braemore
Satnav: KW6 6EX   **Start GR:** ND 073304   **High Point GR:** ND 005285
OS Map: Landranger 17 Helmsdale & Strath of Kildonan
Distance: 15km   **Ascent:** 560m   **Time:** 7.5hrs
Cafe/Pub: La Mirage, Helmsdale (01431 821615, www.lamirage.org).

Directions

Start from the phone box which is 500m W of Braemore, and 9km along the minor road which goes W from Dunbeath. There are a few parking places at this spot, which is just before the road crosses Berriedale Water.

Cross the bridge and then follow the road W for 500m to Braeval. Continue W through the farmyard and W then WSW along a bridleway for 3.5km, until just S of Corrichoich. There are dramatic views S along this stretch towards the conical, vertiginous Maiden Pap.

Follow the path SSW for 2km to the bealach between Morven and Carn Mor; after approximately 500m this path becomes indistinct. As you approach Morven it will seem that the routes up the mountain are quite forbidding, as the mountain is steep, strewn with boulders and seemingly without paths. After reaching the bealach, head 700m SW around the base of Morven until you are on a line between Morven's summit and the homesteads (sheepfold and aisled house) which are approximately 1km S of the bealach. From this point a path goes steeply NW up Morven through a heather gully with fields of stones either side of it. There are a couple of big rocks towards the top – thereafter the gradient reduces in the final 300m. Morven's summit is unmarked, but obvious, and can be very windy!

Return by the same route.

Nearby

You've come this far north, so why not travel a little further and visit John o'Groats? Although not quite the most northerly point on the British mainland (see opposite) and not a particularly attractive place (it received an award for being 'Scotland's most dismal town' in 2010), it's still one end of the Land's End-John o'Groats traverse!

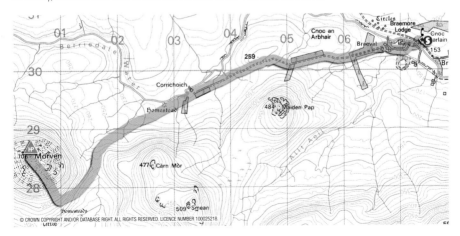

Great Chishill_#83

146m | 479ft   24ᵗʰ | 06/09/08 | with Alex

Cambridgeshire is known for many things – its world-class university, its fenlands and its 'Silicon Fen' cluster of high-tech businesses – but not for its county top! Given that much of Cambridgeshire is dominated by The Fens – a flat, marshy region – it is unsurprising that this county top is rather unremarkable and indeed barely discernible. (At 146 metres above sea-level, it is little more than a tenth the height of Ben Nevis.) This top is Great Chishill, close to Cambridgeshire's border with Essex and celebrated by nothing more than an unmarked tree in a field. A few yards from a road, all you have to do to visit it is to drive by ...

Cambridgeshire itself is far from unremarkable, however, and has plenty to offer visitors. Most obvious is Cambridge, famed for its university, punts and stunning architecture. Away from that, it plays host to a number of festivals and events (such as the Midsummer Fair, which dates back to the 11th century) and is home to The Eagle – the pub in which James Watson and Francis Crick first announced their discovery of the 'secret of life' – DNA. Cambridge is also the centre of the 'Silicon Fen', the name given (with a nod to Silicon Valley in California) to the large number of high-tech industries clustered around the area, which is now one of the most important technological centres in Europe.

In a book detailing the whereabouts of the highest points in all the counties of Britain, one might overlook the fact that each county must also have a low point. In the case of modern-day Cambridgeshire, that low point is rather special. At nine feet below sea level, Holme Fen is the lowest point in the country. See page 262.

Start/parking: B1309 by The Hall

Satnav: GREAT CHISHILL	Start GR: TL 428384	High Point GR: TL 428384

OS Map: Landranger 154 Cambridge & Newmarket

Distance: N/A	Ascent: N/A	Time: N/A

Cafe/Pub: The Pheasant in Great Chishill is worth a visit (01763 838535).

Directions

Start in Great Chishill, on the verge of the B1039 just where the road's direction turns from SE to E. This is by The Hall.

Step out of the car and view the high point! The top is unmarked and is the site of a tree in the field just to the N of the road. The Essex county top – Chrishall Common – is close by, just 2.5km to the SE (see p116).

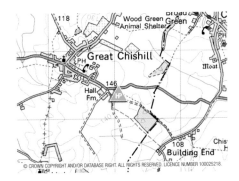

Nearby

The Wicken Fen wetland nature reserve (www.wicken.org.uk), the first reserve acquired by the National Trust (in 1899) and a Site of Special Scientific Interest. There's also the Imperial War Museum at Duxford, reputedly Britain's largest aviation museum (www.iwm.org.uk/visits/iwm-duxford).

▲ THE TREE MARKS GREAT CHISHILL 'SUMMIT'

Plynlimon_#29

752m | 2,467ft

65th | 20/05/10 | solo

Cardiganshire is in my mind notable for the small town of Cardigan, where about 4,000 people live. I found Cardigan a very buzzy place and, wondering why, realised that it is full of independent shops, only a few supermarkets and has an unusual number of butchers, bakers, greengrocers, ironmongers and the like. This might perhaps seem a small matter but it appears that the type of shops in a town are in some way a barometer of its attractiveness. My experience, consistently across the country, is that those (sadly many) towns where independent shops have largely disappeared are without exception towns which seem unattractive, bland or without energy or interest. So I conclude localism matters greatly to this country, much more than I had imagined before I started my *High Point* project – and it is at the heart of what makes Britain so attractive to so many people. Other good examples in Wales are Hay-on-Wye, Dolgellau and Conwy.

The interestingly-named Plynlimon (anglicised from the Welsh *Pumlumon*) has a mystical quality about it. This may be because it is a kind of southern outrider to the imposing mountains of Snowdonia or perhaps because, if folklore is to be believed, there is a sleeping giant beneath its grassy slopes. Whether this is true or not, the peak is the highest point in Mid Wales and in the Cambrian Mountains, and is the source of the longest river in Britain, the Severn.

From the map it seemed the walk would be unremarkable, a yomp up a grassy slope. It turned out to be much more than that. The vista from the top was spectacular, which was a pleasant surprise as the top had been in cloud for almost all of the walk up. An even more pleasant surprise though was to approach Llyn Llygad Rheidol and discover the superb view of Plynlimon's north face – a lovely remote spot, made even more so as I came across just two people all day.

Start/parking: Car park at S end of Nant-y-moch Reservoir, from minor road off A44

Satnav: SY23 3AD (Ponterwyd, nearest)   **Start GR:** SN 756862   **High Point GR:** SN 789869

OS Map: Landranger 135 Aberystwyth & Machynlleth

Distance: 11km   **Ascent:** 400m   **Time:** 5hrs

Cafe/Pub: Pleasant tea and cakes can be had in the tea rooms of the Woodlands Caravan park, at Devil's Bridge on the A4120 road above the pretty Rheidol valley (01970 890233).

Directions

Start from the car park at the dam by the S end of the Nant-y-moch Reservoir. This is 8km N on the minor road which leads from Ponterwyd on the A44.

Follow the road NE for 2km, until you are 400m past the pumping station where Nant-y-moch stream meets the reservoir. Take the track which heads S then NE from this point. Follow the track for 1km until it crosses the Maesnant stream. Then head SE, then E along the N side of the stream; there is a path up here, not marked on the map, but it comes and goes as you move up it. Continue until near the 668m spot point then head S for 500m up Plynlimon. The top is a trig point. The slopes are all quite short grass on this route.

Return via the Llyn Llygad Rheidol reservoir. Follow the N side of the fence E then ENE for 1km until reaching the cairn at the 727m spot point. Head NE for 500m until reaching the stone by the fence just NE of the 724m spot point. Follow the W side of the fence NW for 500m and then head down W along Nant y Graig-las for 700m until reaching the reservoir. The views of Plynlimon's N face are superb from here. Skirt the N side of the reservoir and follow the track NW then SW for 2.5km back to the road.

Nearby

20 kilometres west are the superb Borth Sands, which stretch for five kilometres north to the River Dovey. Walking on them at low tide – when the remains of an ancient submerged forest, said to be part of the sunken kingdom of Cantre'r Gwaelod, can be seen – is a memorable experience.

▲ PLYNLIMON'S NORTH FACE

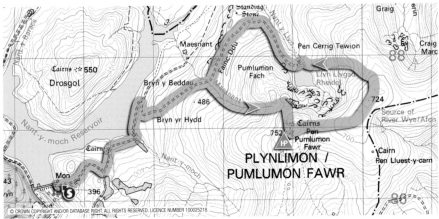

Fan Foel_#27

781m | 2,562ft

55th | 06/10/09 | solo

Carmarthenshire seems to be a county little-known to people outside Wales. It has very green countryside with a patchwork quilt of small and strangely shaped fields. Three rivers (Taf, Teifi and Tywi) and many castles (which date back almost a millennium, to the days of Welsh icon Owain Glyndwr, who some see as the father of current-day Welsh nationalism) provide extra interest for the visitor.

The county top of Carmarthenshire, Fan Foel, is not actually a peak in its own right, instead being a subsidiary summit of the 802-metre-high Fan Brycheiniog, sitting some 20 metres lower than its 'parent'. Crucially, it is also a short distance to the north-west of Fan Brycheiniog – putting the two on different sides of the county boundary with Brecknockshire.

Carmarthenshire is the third largest county in Wales, and the largest of the historic counties. Somewhat mountainous in nature, especially in the north and east where it runs into the Cambrian Mountains and Brecon Beacons respectively, it is a very fertile county and is occasionally known as 'the garden of Wales'. Perhaps this fertility is due in part to the weather: Fan Foel was one of my wettest walks and it rained heavily all day. The summit plateau was in cloud, which was disappointing as I had anticipated lovely views to the east across the Brecon Beacons. Fortunately the route was reasonably straightforward to navigate in the conditions. I saw no one all day other than a school expedition group of eight.

Start/parking: Road verge north of Pencarreg

Satnav: SA19 9UL (nearest)　　**Start GR:** SN 782245　　　**High Point GR:** SN 821223

OS Map: Landranger 160 Brecon Beacons

Distance: 12km　　　**Ascent:** 500m　　　**Time:** 5.5hrs

Cafe/Pub: None close by, but there are options in Llangagog and Llandeilo.

▲ LOOKING SOUTH FROM NEAR PENCARREG

▲ FAN FOEL SUMMIT

Directions

Start from just north of Pencarreg on the verge of the mainly single track minor road which is the Beacons Way. This is a tricky spot to find a parking space, 1km E of the Red Lion YHA Hostel in Llandeussant and 5km E of Pont Newydd, which is on the A4069 5km SE of Llangadog. An alternative is to continue for 1.5km, past Blaenau, but this is less certain.

Follow the road ESE for 700m until it forks. Take the right fork down to a bridge and then follow the Beacons Way route SSE up the hillside to the 677m spot height on Waun Lefrith.

An alternative but less pleasant route to here is to take the left fork rather than the right and to continue on the road past Blaenau for 2.5km up to the dam at Llyn y Fan Fach; then go up the hill W for 500m to the Beacons Way and S 500m to the 677m spot height at Waun Lefrith.

Then walk along the Bannau Sir Gaer cliff top NE for 3km to the top at Fan Foel. The top is a cairn, not to be confused with the trig point 500m SE at Fan Brycheiniog.

Nearby

I particularly enjoyed visiting Dylan Thomas's house in Laugharne, where he wrote much of his poetry. With an exhibition to Thomas, a tearoom and stunning views out over the Taf estuary, it's well worth a trip. www.dylanthomasboathouse.com

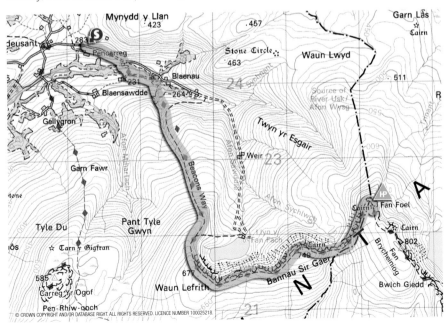

Shining Tor_#46

559m | 1,834ft   22nd | 22/08/08 | solo

Cheshire – home to an observatory with one of the world's largest radio telescopes, one of the best-preserved walled cities in the UK and Britain's oldest cheese.

The observatory is Jodrell Bank, a huge installation which has played a key role in space research. It has a number of huge telescopes in operation, including the 250-foot Lovell Telescope. Completed in 1957 (using gun turrets from Navy Battleships) it was the largest 'steerable dish' radio telescope in the world at the time (it's now number three) and was used to track Sputnik – the world's first man-made satellite.

The walled county town, Chester, has a number of fine medieval buildings – although several of the black-timbered houses in the centre are actually of Victorian origin. The centre is surrounded by Chester City Walls, a defensive rampart first constructed by the Romans and developed by the Normans and by Royalists in the civil war. Today, it's possible to walk the walls, which are well worth a visit.

Cheshire cheese, meanwhile, may not be as popular as Cheddar – which accounts for over 50 per cent of all cheese sales in the UK – but is one of the oldest cheeses in the country, with the British Cheese Board suggesting that it is mentioned in the Domesday Book. You can find traditional Cheshire cheeses throughout the county – particularly at farmers' markets – or visit Nantwich museum, which has an exhibition dedicated to cheese-making.

Shining Tor is on Cheshire's eastern boundary and has superb views north towards Manchester, Jodrell Bank and, if you're lucky, North Wales. To the east, they stretch towards the Derbyshire Peak District. The walk to the top is easy, following a well-defined path along a broad, heathery, peaty ridge – a lovely route which for some reason exceeded my expectations. And yet, on the day I visited, I met no one. It would make an excellent Sunday outing for anybody living between Manchester and Stoke. Don't stray too far into the peat bogs on the western sides of the hill though – they're thought to be several metres deep!

Start/parking: Car park north of Oldgate Nick

Satnav: Kettleshulme (nearest)	**Start GR:** SJ 994767	**High Point GR:** SJ 994737
OS Map: Landranger 118 Stoke-on-Trent & Macclesfield		
Distance: 6km	**Ascent:** 80m	**Time:** 2.5hrs
Cafe/Pub: Cat & Fiddle Inn, on the A537 Buxton–Macclesfield road (01298 78366).		

Directions

Start from the car park by a junction of minor roads just N of Oldgate Nick. This is 3km S of Kettleshulme and 2km W of Errwood Reservoir.

Cross the road and follow the track S over moorland for 3km along a ridge over Cats Tor and onward to Shining Tor. The top is a trig point.

Nearby

Eight kilometres south-east is the interesting spa town of Buxton. Visit the extensive limestone caves of Poole's Cavern, St Ann's Well (where Buxton mineral water is bottled) or the fine Opera House for musical and theatrical entertainment.
www.visitbuxton.co.uk

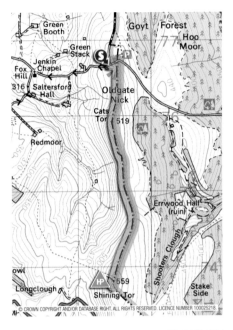

▲ SHINING TOR SUMMIT TRIG POINT

Clackmannanshire

Ben Cleuch_#33

721m | 2,365ft   34th | 06/03/09 | with Annie and Charlie

Clackmannanshire is the smallest historic county in Scotland and in the UK (in terms of area) – less than half as big as England's smallest, Rutland, and a third the size of Flintshire in Wales. The highpoint, Ben Cleuch, is relatively tall, being also the highest point in the Ochil Hills, which stretch along the Ochil fault line from Scotland's east coast to Stirling. They cross the top of Clackmannanshire, rising wall-like from its flat plains in a 400-metre-high escarpment topped by a high plateau which is cut by burns and streams into steep-sided valleys and gullies.

My trip up Ben Cleuch began in the wonderfully-named small town of Tillicoultry – a name that somehow conveys something special. The name derives from an anglicised version of the Scots Gaelic Tulach Cultraidh and translates as 'the mount or hill at the back of the country' – a rather fitting title. This was my first walk involving a significant amount of snow, and was also special as it was my first high point walk with my daughter Annie and her friend (now fiancé!) Charlie. The walk was very steep, up grassy slopes until the last mile when the gradient eased but the snow appeared (about a foot deep at the top). We pressed on regardless of the snow as the route was easy to navigate. From the top we could see right down towards Edinburgh, with the shimmering sun reflected in the Firth of Forth.

I experienced a bit of a surreal city vs. county situation on Ben Cleuch. When we had our lunch on the mountain it turned out that my companions Annie and Charlie, who had bought their lunch in a shop in Waverley railway station, had brought with them hoisin duck wraps and sushi. My guess is that was a first on Ben Cleuch, and it was a far cry from my more conventional mountain diet of nuts and dried fruit!

Start/parking: Park in the side-streets in Tillicoultry

Satnav: FK13 6DP	**Start GR:** NS 914974	**High Point GR:** NN 902006
OS Map: Landranger 58 Perth & Alloa		
Distance: 7.5km	**Ascent:** 720m	**Time:** 5.5hrs

Cafe/Pub: Tilly's Tearoom in Tillicoultry, a good tea spot (01259 752642, www.tillytearoom.co.uk).

Directions

Start from the (delightfully named) Tillicoultry.

From the W end of Tillicoultry, follow the river N. At the end of the built up area, follow the path which skirts the E side of the woods and then goes NW across open land up Mill Glen. Shortly after the intersection of Daiglen Burn and Gannel Burn, follow the path N, sharply up over the grassy slopes towards and up The Law; it is 1.5km from the intersection of the burns to the top of The Law. Follow the W side of the fence N for 700m. When the fence meets two others at a three way intersection, follow the left fence WNW for 600m up to the top of Ben Cleuch. The top is a trig point.

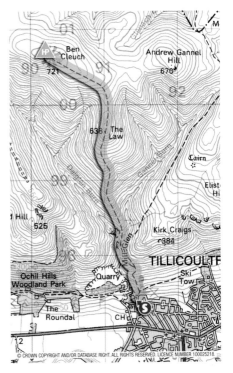

Nearby

Visit the pretty town of Stirling, a short distance west. Full of history, shops, cafes, walks ... the list goes on! www.visitstirling.org

▲ LOOKING SOUTH-EAST OVER THE OCHIL HILLS TOWARDS THE FIRTH OF FORTH AND EDINBURGH

Brown Willy_#60

420m | 1,378ft   31ˢᵗ | 16/10/08 | solo

Cornwall: the first – or final – county in Britain, is a county with a very distinctive character, and is a special place for me as I must have had nearly twenty holidays there over the years. A mention of Cornwall instantly conjures up countless images of rocky coastlines, coastal footpath walks and colourful fishing villages with harbours full of boats. There are the bright skies, narrow lanes with high grassy fences and National Trust holiday cottages. And food: cream teas, saffron bread and Cornish pasties. In recent years it also conjures up images of the copper mines in east Cornwall, where some of my ancestors worked in the mid-nineteenth century (at that time Cornwall produced half of the world's copper).

In the middle of Cornwall is Bodmin Moor, where you'll find the county top – Brown Willy. The most southerly county top in the UK; it's also one with a rather silly name – although when a recent campaign pushed to change the name to 'Bronn Wennili' – Cornish for 'Hill of Swallows' – it was rejected by Cornish residents. Lying inside a Site of Special Scientific Interest (SSSI) on Bodmin Moor, Brown Willy is a 420-metre high tor, surrounded by barren marshy moorland.

The route to the top is over grassy, but not tricky, moorland. During my visit, on a windy, showery day, this felt rather tedious – until I reached the top and was treated to a seemingly endless vista of delightful autumn colours and the unusual sight of rain showers being blown across the county down below. These showers may have been part of the 'Brown Willy effect' – a meteorogical phenomenon where heavy showers develop over high ground on Bodmin Moor and are then carried away by the wind. When the weather forecasters say there will be showers, I now have a new insight into what that really means!

Start/parking: Poldue Downs car park

Satnav: PL32 9QG	**Start GR:** SX 138818	**High Point GR:** SX 158800
OS Map: Landranger 201 Plymouth & Launceston		
Distance: 6km	**Ascent:** 240m	**Time:** 3hrs

Cafe/Pub: Various tea options in the interesting town of Launceston, and good beer and dinner at the Mill House Inn at nearby Trebarwith (01840 770200, www.themillhouseinn.co.uk).

Directions

Start from the Poldue Downs car park at the end of the minor road 3km SE of Camelford.

Follow the track SE across a stream and on to open grassy land. Head SE steadily up the hill for 1.2km until in the region of Showery Tor. Go SW for 500m along the top of the hill to Rough Tor. There are splendid views from here and interesting, windswept rocks.

Retrace your steps to Showery Tor, then drop down SSE for 500m to the stream below. Pick up the path E from here and follow it E then SE for 600m to Brown Willy. The top is a trig point.

Nearby

Tintagel, on the coast, is one of the most-visited places in the county. A dramatic castle on a beautiful stretch of coastline, it is said to be the birthplace of King Arthur.

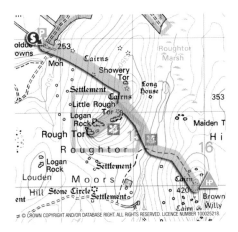

▲ BROWN WILLY SUMMIT

▲ LOOKING OVER CORNWALL FROM ROUGH TOR

Burnhope Seat_#30

747m | 2,451ft   67th | 14/06/10 | with Tim and Anne

County Durham's high point is Burnhope Seat, right on the boundary with Cumbria in the North Pennines, which are the most remote, empty and bleak part of England – altogether different from the territory further south in the Pennines. There's seemingly nothing here. From the hilltops there are no villages or roads to be seen and few trees – just open moorland. Indeed, the northern Pennines are truly England's most remote land, the bare hillsides being frequently described as 'England's last wilderness'.

Burnhope Seat is no exception, sitting at the head of Teesdale (which is a delightful valley), its top is a huge, bare peat moor. The area surrounding the hill has a few ski tows and many shake holes and disused mine workings, but little else. It seems truly empty, despite the fact that a road passes within about a kilometre of the summit. The overall feeling in the area is one of open moorland and wonderful head-of-the-valley remoteness along the spine of the Pennines.

I have family connections in the area, as my mother was brought up in Weardale, the next valley to the north, in the 1920s and 1930s. So it was interesting to get a sense of the area, which must have felt very remote at that time; indeed I recall hearing various stories of when her village was cut off by snow in winter. Further to the east, her ancestors had been coal miners in the (now closed) Murton Colliery, which was very interesting to visit on its annual open day. My brother Tim and his wife Anne accompanied me on my walk, and we came across no one all day. Towards the top the ground got very boggy underfoot (and, bizarrely, we came across various frogs).

From the summit, we could see Mickle Fell (old Yorkshire high point, p254). Little did I know the trouble I would have there later on.

Start/parking: The B6277 10km SSE of Alston

Satnav: CA9 3DS	Start GR: NY 774365	High Point GR: NY 787375
OS Map: Landranger 92 Barnard Castle & Richmond		
Distance: 4km	Ascent: 170m	Time: 2hrs

Cafe/Pub: Cafes in Alston and Middleton in Teesdale. Or the Village Bakery in Melmerby, 15km SW of Alston, a pleasant cafe and gallery (www.village-bakery.com).

Directions

Start from the W side of the B6277 10km SSE of Alston, 0.2km north of the milestone marked on the map, and shortly before the road heads down towards Middleton in Teesdale.

Follow the road S to the milestone and then head NE and climb for 1.5km to the summit of Burnhope Seat. There is a fence which goes broadly NW from Burnhope Seat, and this can be a useful tool in locating the summit. Towards the top the ground gets very boggy underfoot. The top is a trig point.

Nearby

Visit Alston and Middleton in Teesdale, which are pleasant little towns. Also visit Barnard Castle, an interesting market town named after its twelfth-century founder, Bernard de Balliol, before the castle later passed into the hands of King Richard III. The Bowes Museum in Barnard Castle has a nationally renowned art collection, housed in a magnificent French-style chateau. Further afield, visit Durham, whose cathedral and castle are UNESCO World Heritage Sites.

▲ WITH TIM ON BURNHOPE SEAT SUMMIT

▲ LOOKING EAST TOWARDS WEARDALE

Scafell Pike_ #10

978m | 3,209ft   54th | 02/09/09 | with Tim

Although the county of Cumberland was abolished, as so many were, under the
Local Government Act of 1972 (see page 10), its name lives on – most obviously in
the modern-day county of Cumbria, of which Cumberland forms the largest part.
But there is also the Cumberland sausage, made of pork, flavoured with herbs and
curled around the plate, and in *HMS Cumberland*, in service with the Royal Navy from
1989 to 2011 and (rather obviously) nicknamed 'The Fighting Sausage'.

But there's more to Cumberland than namesakes. With much of the Lake District
National Park within its borders, the area is rightly feted for the loveliness of its landscapes,
which are undeniably beautiful and special. It is, however, busy as a result, and its most
noted mountains are popular and well-walked; if you are seeking remoteness in Cumbria
you have to be quite savvy to find it and you will have to look past the honeypot locations.

Scafell Pike is one of these honeypots and notable as it is, at 978 metres, England's
highest mountain. Distinct from, but often confused with, its neighbour Sca Fell (to which it
is connected by a rocky col), the summit is a grey boulderfield which offers fantastic views
out across the Lake District.

Seathwaite, where we started our walk, claims to be the wettest inhabited place in
England, receiving about 140 inches of rain per annum. If the weather that day was in any
way typical, I can well believe that claim! I climbed Scafell Pike with my brother Tim on one
of the wettest days of all my trips. Notwithstanding this, the day was memorable as the
Lake District scenery is amongst the most beautiful in Britain, and the colours were superb
in the wet. We saw only a few people during the day except at the top, which was quite
busy. The route was quite tricky in its last stretch, before the final summit push, as it was
across piled up, quite sharp boulders, which were slippery in the wet.

Start/parking: Car park near Seathwaite

Satnav: CA12 5XJ	**Start GR:** NY 236123	**High Point GR:** NY 215072
OS Map: Landranger 89 West Cumbria; Landranger 90 Penrith & Keswick		
Distance: 13km	**Ascent:** 860m	**Time:** 8.5hrs

Cafe/Pub: There are pubs and cafes dotted around Borrowdale. Try the Langstrath Country Inn
in Seathwaite (017687 77239, www.thelangstrath.com).

Directions

Start from the car park which is on the E
verge at the S end of the road from Seatoller
(in Borrowdale) to Seathwaite.

Follow the track for 1.5km S through the
farm buildings and along the E side of the
river to Stockley Bridge. Cross the bridge over
Grains Gill and continue S and then SSW for
2km – this goes steadily upwards until it
meets the bridleway from Sprinkling Tarn to
Angle Tarn. Then bear SE for 700m until the
crossroads at Esk Hause. Head W upwards
for 800m and then SW for 1.5km to Scafell
Pike; this last stretch is across piled up, quite
sharp boulders and can be tricky in the wet.
The path rises steeply before reaching the
summit. The top is a trig point, where you
will in all probability find many other walkers.

Return the same way as far as Esk Hause.
Then walk NW for 2km down past Sprinkling
Tarn as far as Sty Head, where there are
superb views. Take the footpath NE past
Styhead Tarn and along (and crossing)
Styhead Gill for 2.5km to Stockley Bridge.
Then cross the bridge and head N back
to Seathwaite.

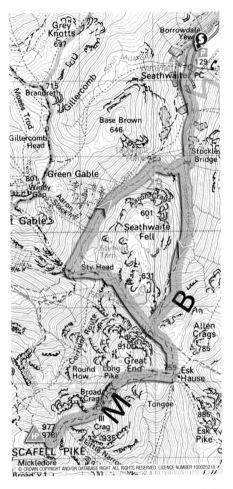

Nearby

A tempting thought is to climb all the
Wainwrights – the 214 'distinct' peaks within
the Lake District National Park over 1,000 feet
high and mentioned in Alfred Wainwright's
famous seven-volume *A Pictorial Guide to
the Lakeland Fells*. Now that would be quite
a project, notwithstanding that several
hundred people have already achieved it.
Maybe that is for another day ...

▲ STYHEAD TARN FROM STY HEAD

Cadair Berwyn_#20

827m | 2,713ft   50th | 05/08/09 | with Joe

Denbighshire has the unusual distinction in Wales of being the name of both a historic and a modern county. The two have very different borders, with the historic county reaching much further west, but both contain the same significant ranges of hills – the Clwyds in the north and the Berwyns in the south. Both are beautiful areas in which to walk and explore; the Clwyds are the smaller of the two, with more woodland and less high ground (but still with a county top: Moel Famau, on the border between Denbighshire and Flintshire), while the Berwyns are bigger and wilder.

Big, bleak and sparsely populated, the Berwyns are a huge open expanse of ground stretching across a sizeable chunk of north-east Wales. The hills and mountains in the area are high, rocky and bare, with a deep covering of heather in the summer. Nearly twenty-five of the Berwyn peaks top 600 metres, including the county top, Cadair Berwyn, which is the highest point in Wales outside the national parks. It's a beautiful, wild area, with fantastic scenery and a whole range of wildlife from peregrine falcons to polecats. Birdwatchers might like to note that the Berwyns are designated a Special Protection Area due to the internationally-significant populations of hen harrier, peregrine and red kite.

The walk to Cadair Berwyn is a delightful one. The most special part of the route is undoubtedly the Pistyll Rhaeadr (Rhaeadr Falls) at the start. These fall in total some 240 feet and, whilst not being the largest waterfalls in Britain (the largest being over twice as high in Assynt, Scotland), they are the most impressive which I have seen and are certainly worth a visit. The walk later passes via Moel Sych (Montgomeryshire's high point) where, on the day of my visit, there were superb 360-degree views for miles around.

Start/parking: Pistyll Rhaeadr car park

Satnav: SY10 0BZ	Start GR: SJ 075294	High Point GR: SJ 072327
OS Map: Landranger 125 Bala & Lake Vyrnwy		
Distance: 7km	Ascent: 530m	Time: 4hrs
Cafe/Pub: Tan-y-Pistyll Cafe, Pistyll Rhaeadr (01691 780392, www.pistyllrhaeadr.co.uk).		

Nearby

200 metres north-west of the car park is the very impressive Pistyll Rhaeadr. This spectacular waterfall, the highest in Wales, drops 240 feet into the Afon Rhaeadr. There is a nice little cafe at the base – perfect for a cup of tea after your walk.

Directions

Start from the car park at Pistyll Rhaeadr, at the end of the minor road from Llanrhaeadr-ym -Mochnant. The map shows that there is a car park 300 metres before the end of the road, but you can in fact park at the very end too.

Follow the path from the car park NE and upwards through the woods. Shortly after the woods, the path turns N and then steeply up NW. Follow the route NW upwards, past Trum Felen up the grassy slopes to the 691m spot point. Then continue NNW upwards by the side of a fence to Moel Sych. The top is a cairn. The distance from the car park is approx. 2.5km. From Moel Sych, follow the path NE for 1km across the grassy top to Cadair Berwyn. The top is a trig point.

Return towards Moel Sych, to a path at the top of the Craig y Llyn cliffs (200m E of Moel Sych). Follow the clifftops down SSE and then E down the ridge which goes just S of Llyn Lluncaws as far as the Nant y Llyn stream; this is 1km from Moel Sych. Follow the path SSE along the stream. After a further 500m the path crosses the stream and then leaves it. Follow the path along, then down the E side of the valley for 2km until it reaches the road, 800m SE of the car park. Follow the road back to the car park. It is tempting to think you can cut the corner and avoid the last 1km or so, but this is hard to do.

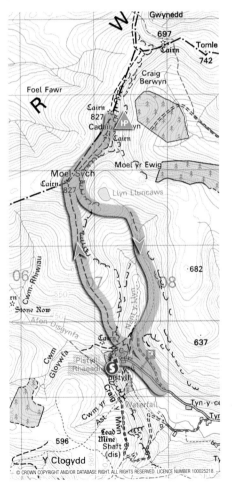

▲ JOE AND BERTIE ON TOP OF CADAIR BERWYN

▲ LOOKING DOWN CWM MAEN GWYNEDD FROM CADAIR BERWYN

Derbyshire

Kinder Scout_ #42

636m | 2,087ft

79th | 08/04/11 | solo

It was due to the events that took place on the county top of Derbyshire in 1932 that we can today walk so freely in the hills. In April of that year, 500 people walked onto Kinder Scout in an act of mass trespass, battling with police and gamekeepers as they went. Prior to that point, much of the British countryside was privately owned, and ordinary people were denied access. The Kinder Trespass began the movement towards the open access we enjoy today.

I first went to Derbyshire in the 1960s, as a teenager on my Duke of Edinburgh Silver Award expedition: thirty miles over three days, starting in Matlock and finishing in Chesterfield. This walk took me across the Derbyshire Peak District, of which Kinder Scout is the highest point. Perfect for weekend breaks and a kind of fresh air lung for the nearby cities of Manchester, Sheffield, Derby and Nottingham, the Peak District is a lovely area. The first designated National Park in the UK, it is a remarkable place, with the bleak moorland and dark gritstone crags of its northern half (the Dark Peak) contrasting sharply with the limestone valleys and green fields further south (the White Peak).

Kinder is famous for its peat bogs – the plateau atop the hill is essentially one huge peaty mass on which navigation is tricky and walking-boot-loss a high possibility! Flowing from its west side is the Kinder Downfall – the tallest waterfall in the Peak (and which, with enough wind, can blow into an 'upfall' several metres high). I opted not to cross the Kinder Scout moor as I was walking alone, so approached the high point from the south. This enabled me to do a lovely circuit along the edge of Edale moor, which has wonderful views to the south. There were quite a few walkers out that day.

Start/parking: Edale village pay and display (or take the train)

Satnav: S33 7ZP   **Start GR:** SK 124853   **High Point GR:** SK 086875

OS Map: Explorer OL1 The Peak District – Dark Peak Area

Distance: 13km   **Ascent:** 400m   **Time:** 5.5hrs

Cafe/Pub: The Pennypot Cafe by the railway station (01433 670293), or The Rambler Inn, Edale (01433 670268, www.theramblerinn.com).

Nearby

Visit the award-winning Chatsworth House Farm Shop in Pilsley (www.chatsworth.org/farmshop) and the superb David Mellor design building just south of Hathersage (www.davidmellordesign.com) – this includes the architecturally iconic Round Building (which is a circular cutlery factory), together with an interesting design museum, high quality shop and cafe.

Directions

Start from Edale. (Edale can be reached by train from Manchester or Sheffield.)

From the station or car park, walk N into the village to find the start of the Pennine Way, which is in the centre of Edale. Follow the Pennine Way WSW for 2km across fields to Upper Booth. Turn WNW along the bridleway, reaching Jacob's Ladder (a stone footpath) after 1.5km. Follow the PW path 700m W and then 700m N to Kinder Low, which is the official summit of the Kinder Scout moor. The top is a trig point.

Return via the southern edge of Kinder Scout to Edale. This is an excellent circular route. Retrace your steps S for 700m to a large cairn where the path diverges. Head NE for 700m past Noe Stool and then generally E for some 5km along the edge of the moor, from which there are superb views S. The path passes the Woolpacks (rocks shaped like woolpacks), Crowden Tower, and the heads of the lovely Crowden Brook and Grinds Brook valleys.

Continue along the moor's edge as far as Nether Tor, just above Golden Clough. Then take the path S for 1km to The Nab, and then SW via zigzags for 1km back down to Edale. The Rambler Inn towards the S of Edale, on the way back to the station, has a pleasant lawn on which to sip a pint of beer.

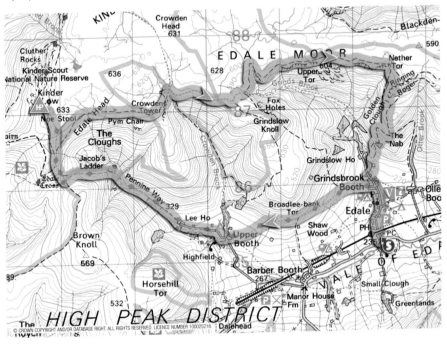

▲ LOOKING DOWN GRINDSBROOK CLOUGH FROM EDALE MOOR

High Willhays_#43

621m | 2,037ft   32ⁿᵈ | 16/10/08 | solo

Stretching across south-west England, Devon is unusual in having both a north and a south coastline. Containing everything from fishing villages to large cities and sandy beaches to wild moorland, it is a wonderfully diverse county and justifiably popular with tourists.

High Willhays is the highest point in England south of Birmingham – although only just: the nearby Yes Tor, which many people mistake as Devon's high point, is only five feet lower. The two peaks form a kilometre-long ridge on north Dartmoor, known as the 'Roof of Devon', with one tor at either end. It should be said that High Willhays is the less impressive of the two, being little more than a few outcrops of rock and a cairn. The majority of Dartmoor's tors – including Yes Tor – are far more dramatic. Dartmoor itself is worth an extended visit: a huge expanse of wild moorland dotted with weathered granite boulders and windswept tors, it contains few roads and even fewer houses. On sunny days, when the heather is high and the big, open skies are a deep blue, it's a beautiful place. My trip was rewarded by groups of Dartmoor ponies free-roaming on the moors – a pleasant surprise – and superb views from the top across Dartmoor and a kaleidoscope of subtle autumn colours. If, however, you're out when the thick Dartmoor mists roll in, enveloping everything in clammy greyness and cutting visibility to nothing in an instant, Dartmoor takes on a distinctly spooky air …

The walk up to High Willhays is straightforward, albeit, after the initial section, not on a path. It is however somewhat hazardous as the route goes through the MoD's Oakhampton Range and access is restricted at certain times. My walk became a bit problematic halfway up, when I came across a line of 'Danger Area' signposts. Nothing seemed to be happening, so I ignored them – although I did tread warily. When I got back to the start, I discovered a notice which said the hill was closed to visitors that month! Unsurprisingly, (or luckily), I came across no one all day.

Start/parking: Car park near Meldon reservoir

Satnav: EX20 4LU (nearest)	**Start GR:** SX 561917	**High Point GR:** SX 580892
OS Map: Landranger 191 Okehampton & North Dartmoor		
Distance: 8km	**Ascent:** 370m	**Time:** 4hrs

Cafe/Pub: Excellent coffee and cakes at the airy New Forge Tea Room in nearby Chagford (01647 433226).

Directions

Start from the car park just to the N of Meldon Reservoir, approximately 5km SW of Okehampton. The route goes through the British Army's Okehampton Range danger area – so check in advance that the area is not restricted on the day of your visit (call free 0800 4584868).

Follow the road SE over the reservoir dam and then go SW for 300m along the track by the reservoir. When the track forks, take the ENE fork up and then S over the grassy slopes of Longstone Hill. Follow the track S for 1km from the top of Longstone Hill. At this point you will be next to the British Army's Okehampton Range danger area (see above re: restrictions on access). Head E for 1.3km up to the summit of Yes Tor, often incorrectly thought to be Dartmoor's highest point, and then SSW and S for 700m along the flat ridge to High Willhays. The top is a large cairn and there are panoramic views across Dartmoor.

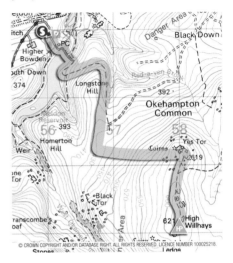

© CROWN COPYRIGHT AND/OR DATABASE RIGHT. ALL RIGHTS RESERVED. LICENCE NUMBER 100025218.

Nearby

Take the road from Tavistock to Moretonhampstead. There are several points along the route where you can park your car and take footpaths to explore Dartmoor more. Then carry on to Chagford, which is a pretty and much visited small town, with good tea shops.

▲ LOOKING OVER DARTMOOR

Lewesdon Hill_#68

279m | 915ft   60ᵗʰ | 27/03/10 | with Alex

Dorset has interested me ever since, as a teenager, I read Thomas Hardy's novels (which are set in Dorset), and discovered that one, *Far From the Madding Crowd*, has a near-namesake character called Mark Clark. The county is dotted with locations used by Hardy, or which inspired him – Weatherby, which features in this novel, is based on Puddletown near Dorset – making Dorset a real fascination for Hardy fans.

   Dorset – formerly known as Dorsetshire – has hosted some significant events in the history of England. It was in Portland Bay in the eighth century that the Vikings first landed in Britain and at the port of Melcombe Regis that the Black Death first arrived on these shores. Nowadays, the Dorset coastline is a little quieter, though no less remarkable. The Jurassic Coastline runs across the bottom of the county – a UNESCO World Heritage Site in which millions of years of geological history can be traced. Complete dinosaur fossils have been found buried within its limestone cliffs and its dramatic coastal arches and stacks are quite a sight. The remainder of the county is rich in pretty countryside and buzzing towns and has a unique character of its own.

   Lewesdon Hill, the high point, is just 279 metres high. The summit was the site of an Iron Age hill fort and the original bank and ditches are still visible. More 'recently' an Armada beacon stood on top of the hill in 1588, ready to be lit in case of a Spanish attack. The hill is an easy walk from Broadwindsor, across sometimes very muddy farmland. We came across no one all day.

Start/parking: Car park in centre of Broadwindsor

Satnav: DT8 3QP	**Start GR:** ST 438025	**High Point GR:** ST 437012

OS Map: Landranger 193 Taunton & Lyme Regis

Distance: 3km	**Ascent:** 130m	**Time:** 1.5hrs

Cafe/Pub: The New Inn, just south of the Levesdon Hill in Stoke Abbot, is a pleasant pub (01308 868333). Alternatively, Hugh Fearnley-Whittingstall's River Cottage Canteen & Deli in nearby Axminster is a good bet, with all sorts of goodies (www.rivercottage.net).

Directions

Start from the car park in the centre of Broadwindsor.

Follow the road W along the B3164 for approximately 300m to a track signposted as a footpath. Follow this S for 200m, and then SE for 200m along the side of a fence. Follow the track, which is sometimes hard to make out, S and then SSE for 1km up to the woods which are along the N side of Lewesdon Hill – the route goes steadily up across open fields, and along the E side of a wood W of Fir Farm. Follow the track S then SE through the woods and up to the summit of Lewesdon Hill. The top is in a grassy clearing and is unmarked.

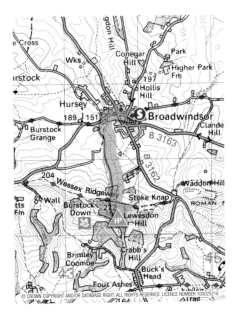

Nearby

Approximately 15 kilometres south-west is the interesting town of Lyme Regis, which has many shops and cafes, the famous Cobb breakwater (famously depicted in the film *The French Lieutenant's Woman*) and gives good access to the Jurassic Coast. Also visit Chesil beach, an 18-mile long pebble beach which runs from near Bridport to Weymouth; Sherborne, a pretty town with a fine abbey and many independent shops and tea shops – try Oliver's Coffee House in Cheap Street and the Town Mill bakery at The Green, both of which I found to be excellent; Gold Hill in Shaftesbury, where the famous old Hovis advert was filmed.

▲ ON LEWESDON HILL

White Coomb_#22

821m | 2,694ft   42nd | 30/04/09 | solo

Dumfries-shire, in the south of Scotland, is a beautiful county which slopes gently downhill from north to south; from the Southern Uplands to the Solway Firth – on the other side of the which is England, and the Cumbrian Lake District.

The county town is Dumfries, once home to the Scottish 'National Poet' Robert Burns. It was interesting to discover that Dumfries is nicknamed 'Queen of the South', as I had always wondered where the eponymous Scottish football team comes from. Continuing on the sporting theme, it was in Dumfries-shire that the bicycle was invented in 1839, by a man named Kirkpatrick Macmillan. Embarrassingly, three years later a Glasgow newspaper reported an incident in which a man riding a 'velocipede' was fined five shillings after knocking over a pedestrian. This man was, apparently, Mr Macmillan. There is a small museum dedicated to the history of the cycle at Drumlanrig Castle – which is worth a visit in its own right (www.drumlanrigcastle.co.uk).

The county top of Dumfries-shire is White Coomb – the highest point in the beautiful Moffat hills. The top itself is formed by the meeting of several broad ridges that rise steeply out of the valleys below. The route up is, at times, quite steep as a result, and is unmarked. Fortunately it is manageable, albeit quite hard going, although I felt dizzy after my ascent, probably because I had over-exerted myself, having climbed Peebles-shire's Broad Law earlier in the day.

The walk is memorable for the impressive Grey Mare's Tail waterfall, just up from the start of the walk. The fifth-highest fall in the UK, water tumbles some 60 metres down from Tail Burn on its way to Moffat Water below. Tail Burn itself presents the walker with a slight problem as it is tricky to cross in spate without getting wet feet!

Start/parking: Car park at the Grey Mare's Tail visitor centre

Satnav: Moffat (nearest)	**Start GR:** NT 186145	**High Point GR:** NT 163151
OS Map: Landranger 79 Hawick & Eskdale		
Distance: 5km	**Ascent:** 600m	**Time:** 4.5hrs

Cafe/Pub: Try the Glen Cafe, eight kilometres north-east, on the west side of the A708. Overlooking the Loch of the Lowes, it's a beautiful spot for a post-walk cup of tea.

Directions

Start from the Grey Mare's Tail visitor centre car park by the A708 towards the top of Moffat Dale.

Follow the steep track NW just up from the N side of Tail Burn. This passes the impressive Grey Mare's Tail waterfalls. After approximately 1km, ford the burn, which may be tricky (without getting wet) if the burn is full. Thereafter there is no clear path, but the route is manageable – aim to go just N of the fence which goes up for 1.7km W past Upper Tarnberry and on to White Coomb.

Nearby

15 kilometres south-west down the A708 is the interesting town of Moffat, an attractive spa town renowned for its toffee; a good first stop if travelling up the M74 from England.

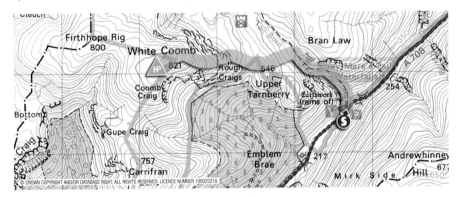

▲ TAIL BURN, WHICH MUST BE CROSSED

▲ LOOKING SOUTH-WEST DOWN MOFFAT DALE

Dunbartonshire

Ben Vorlich (Beinn Mhùrlaig)_#13

943m | 3,094ft

68th | 16/07/10 | solo

There was some family interest in my trip to Dunbartonshire as, just further up Loch Lomond on its east side, a relative of my wife used to live in a cottage in an isolated spot which was only accessible by boat. Such isolation does not feel out of place in Scotland, although it can, at times, be hard to get around Loch Lomond thanks to its ease of access from Glasgow.

Dunbartonshire runs from Dumbarton up the west side of beautiful Loch Lomond in central Scotland. The high point is Ben Vorlich. Sitting at the top of Loch Lomond, it is part of the splendidly-named Arrochar Alps, but sits apart from the rest of the range, between Loch Lomond and the Loch Sloy reservoir. The name Ben Vorlich means 'hill of the bay' in Gaelic and is a name given to a number of peaks across Scotland – the most notable of which are the county top here and the 985-metre high Ben Vorlich in Perthshire. 'Our' Ben Vorlich is one of those Munros on which the route up it is both indistinct and steep – a tricky combination. You have to be alert at the top, particularly in the mist, as the county top is, confusingly, not at the trig point. The top of Ben Vorlich is a ridge with three small summits. The high point is the central summit, while it is the southern one, 200 metres away, which is marked with the trig.

I went up on a wet day with cloud at around the 2,500-feet level. It was disappointing that the top was in cloud as Ben Vorlich is noted for its wonderful views down the length of Loch Lomond. Luckily, I was rewarded on the way down when, just below the cloud line, Loch Lomond appeared beneath me, shimmering like mercury – a lovely surprise.

Start/parking: Inveruglas visitor centre

Satnav: G83 7DP	**Start GR:** NN 322098	**High Point GR:** NN 295124
OS Map: Landranger 56 Loch Lomond & Inveraray		
Distance: 13km	**Ascent:** 930m	**Time:** 8hrs

Cafe/Pub: The Coach House Coffee Shop in Luss (01436 860341).

▲ LOCH LOMOND FROM BEN VORLICH

Directions

Start from the car park of the visitor centre at Inveruglas.

Follow the path SSW along the W side of the A82, until just before the corner where the road turns sharply SE. Take the track W under the railway line and follow it W past the N side of the power station. 500m after the power station, the road turns NW towards the Loch Sloy dam. Approximately 500m before the dam, at a very small, easy to miss, shin-high cairn on the right side of the road, a footpath heads NE up the side of Ben Vorlich. This path, unmarked on the map but quite near a stream which is marked, rises steeply.

Head up NE for 700m until approximately at the 700m contour – the path will come and go as you ascend, but eventually becomes clear. Head 1.5km NW to the top of Ben Vorlich, with superb views S over Loch Lomond. The top is a cairn on a rocky promontory, approximately 200m NNW of the trig point.

Nearby

To the west, on the A83 Inveraray road, is Loch Fyne, noted for its oysters and kippers – and at the top of the loch is an oyster bar and farm shop. Not so nearby (18 kilometres south on the A82) is the Coach House Coffee Shop in the picturesque village of Luss – a good tea spot. Luss is a conservation village (with a kiltmaker and a bagpipe works) with lovely views over Loch Lomond towards Ben Lomond (the Stirlingshire high point), and is a popular spot to visit.

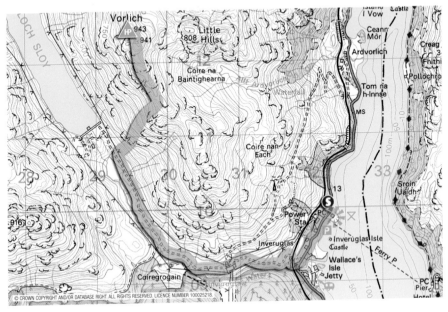

East Lothian

Meikle Says Law_#50

535m | 1,755ft   Joint 57th (shared with Berwickshire) | 22/10/09 | with Alex

East Lothian is one of the smaller Scottish counties, sitting on the east coast, at the end of the Firth of Forth, which forms the northern boundary of the county. It is known for the number and quality of its beaches, and for its fine coastline, popular with holiday makers, watersports enthusiasts and wildlife spotters alike.

Exploring inland, you'll find a particularly picturesque region of Scotland. Hill forts, medieval castles and attractive towns and villages share the landscape with a typically Scottish countryside of forest and, as you move towards the southern boundary, the remote and heathery Lammermuir Hills. These hills are home to the high point, Meikle Says Law, which is on the southern boundary of East Lothian, on the border with Berwickshire and is the shared high point of both counties.

Although they are not particularly high, only one road crosses the Lammermuir Hills, which, with their barren and exposed hilltops and steep hillsides, form a dramatic barrier as one travels north into Scotland. Together with the Moorfoot and Pentland hills to the west, they form a comparatively little-known but lovely part of Scotland.

I already knew East Lothian as my wife's parents used to live there, in a rural spot near Haddington, birthplace of the Scottish icon John Knox. Knox was a sixteenth-century Scottish clergyman who was exiled from the country before returning to lead the Protestant Reformation in Scotland.

Start/parking: On minor road near Faseny Cottage

Satnav: Satnav: GIFFORD (nearest)   Start GR: NT 612636   High Point GR: NT 581617

OS Map: Landranger 67 Duns, Dunbar & Eyemouth

Distance: 8km   Ascent: 190m   Time: 3.5hrs

Cafe/Pub: Try the Victoria Inn, Haddington (01620 823332).

Full details of the walk can be found on p64 for Berwickshire.

Nearby

Visit North Berwick, a buzzy little town on the north coast, and (in the years when The Open is there – last time in 2013) the Muirfield golf links at Gullane. Also visit the John Muir Country Park, just north of Dunbar; John Muir was a noted explorer, naturalist and conservationist born in Dunbar.

▲ ON TOP OF MEIKLE SAYS LAW

Chrishall Common_#82

147m | 482ft   25th | 06/09/08 | with Alex

Essex is one of the older counties in England – dating back to the pre-Norman era. Once a vast county, containing most of the land that later became Middlesex and Hertfordshire, it is today smaller in area, although still the seventh-largest county in England in terms of population. The name Essex originated in Anglo-Saxon times, coming from the Old English 'Ēast Seaxe', meaning the 'East Saxons' (the area was the eastern kingdom of the Saxons). And Colchester in the north-east of the county is Britain's oldest recorded town, dating back to before the Roman conquest, when it was known as *Camulodunum* and was sufficiently well-developed to have its own mint.

Although close to London and correspondingly busy in places, once you move beyond the green belt area outside the city and away from the larger towns of Chelmsford, Colchester and Southend, much of the county is rural, with many small towns, villages and hamlets largely built in the traditional materials of timber and brick, with clay tile or thatched roofs, separated by farmed fields and areas of woodland.

The high point, Chrishall Common, is fairly unremarkable. It is situated near the Cambridgeshire border, on the Harcamlow Way (a 227-kilometre-long footpath in a figure-of-eight shape), relatively close to the Cambridgeshire high point of Great Chishill (p80). You reach the high point across farmland and the top is barely discernible as the area around it is so flat and the approach is through woods. We saw no one on the walk, but had a pleasant surprise when we came across half a dozen Bambi-like deer crossing a field.

Start/parking: Village common in Langley

Satnav: CB11 4RY (approx.)	**Start GR:** TL 446351	**High Point GR:** TL 443362
OS Map: Landranger 154 Cambridge & Newmarket		
Distance: 2.5km	**Ascent:** 20m	**Time:** 1hr

Cafe/Pub: Try The Axe and Compasses in nearby Arkesden (01799 550272).

Directions

Start from the village common in Langley.

Follow the Harcamlow Way NW from the road by the village common. Continue along the side of a field until it crosses the edge of another large field, 500m from the road. Take a path NNE along the side of this field for 400m until it reaches some woods; then follow the SW edge of the woods for 300m and head N through the woods at their narrowest point. On emerging from the woods go 100m to the SW corner of the field. The top is unmarked and is this spot, which is still on the Harcamlow Way.

Nearby

Visit Saffron Walden, a flourishing and historic market town with attractive old buildings. Also visit Audley End House just outside the town. This is a fine Jacobean country house (one of the finest in the country) and well worth a visit.

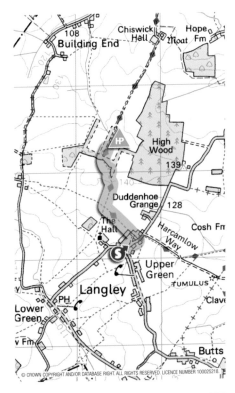

▲ THE FIELDS AT CHRISHALL COMMON

West Lomond_#52

522m | 1,713ft

53ʳᵈ | 17/08/09 | with Alex

Fife, often known as the Kingdom of Fife, is a peninsula jutting out into the sea just north of Edinburgh on the east coast of Scotland. It is bordered to the north by the Firth of Tay and to the south by the Firth of Forth. Predictably, then, Fife is noted for its coastline. It's a delightful coast, well-known for its pretty coastal villages, particularly in the south-east, and popular for its walks, watersports and wildlife. Former Prime Minister Gordon Brown's constituency of Kirkcaldy and Cowdenbeath is on the southern coast of the county and the impressive construction of the cantilever Forth Rail Bridge crosses the Firth of Forth, linking the county to Edinburgh.

Inland, there's some lovely countryside. The highest point in the county is West Lomond, in the Lomond Hills (or 'Paps of Fife'), a relatively small and low range of hills in the centre of the county. Despite their size, they are highly prominent and visible from some distance as they rise dramatically out of flat surroundings and, due to their proximity to several large towns and cities (including Edinburgh), they can become busy with walkers.

West Lomond is easily distinguished – its bare, conical summit rising out of the hills. Its twin, East Lomond, has a similar appearance but is significantly lower, at 424 metres high. The two can be combined in a satisfying and worthwhile walk along the six-and-a-half-kilometre 'ridge' of the Lomond Hills. The West Lomond county top walk is an easy amble until the end, which is very steep but rewards the walker with superb and uninterrupted views out over the surrounding county.

Start/parking: Car park 2.5km SW of Falkland

Satnav: KY6 3HH (nearest)   **Start GR:** NO 227061   **High Point GR:** NO 197066

OS Map: Landranger 58 Perth & Alloa

Distance: 7km   **Ascent:** 220m   **Time:** 3hrs

Cafe/Pub: There are some nice cafes in the nearby attractive former royal burgh of Falkland, or try the Lomond Hills Hotel in Freuchie (01337 857329, www.lomondhillshotel.com).

▲ LOOKING SOUTH-EAST FROM WEST LOMOND

Directions

Start from the car park on the minor road 2.5km SW of Falkland.

Follow the track WNW for 2km across the Lomond Hills and then 1km WSW to West Lomond. West Lomond is a steep hill and the easiest way up is to take the path which skirts the north side and then goes ESE for the last 300m to the summit, from which there are panoramic views. The top is a trig point.

Nearby

Visit St Andrews, a characterful university town and home to the world famous Royal & Ancient Golf Club. The eighteenth tee is easily accessed (it goes right up to the town centre) and is very atmospheric.

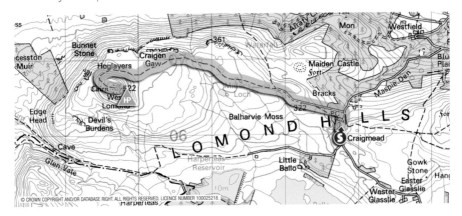

▲ ALEX ON TOP OF WEST LOMOND, WITH EAST LOMOND BEHIND

Moel Famau_#47

554m | 1,818ft   51ˢᵗ | 07/08/09 | with Alex

Flintshire sits in the top right-hand corner of Wales, against the border with England. It's a part of Wales that many people overlook as they speed by en route to the hills of Snowdonia, or to the large towns and cities just over the border in England. In my family, it is recognised as the county whose piece was always missing from the wooden 'British Counties Jigsaw'. It was, then, a lovely surprise to visit Flintshire and discover the Clwydian Hills, which dominate the county's west side.

Upon visiting, I found a very scenic range of purple heather-clad hills, many of which are topped by ancient hill forts, and also the county top, Moel Famau. Lying in an Area of Outstanding Natural Beauty, it is a particularly scenic and popular hill, and Alex and I met many people on our walk to the top. The lower slopes of the hill are quite varied – forest on one side, open grassland on another and scrubby moorland elsewhere. The top of the hill, which is on the Offa's Dyke Path (as is the Herefordshire high point, Black Mountain – p128), is marked by the quite-derelict Jubilee Tower. Built in 1810 to commemorate the golden jubilee of George III, it was to have been topped by an Egyptian-styled obelisk but was never completed.

The walk's start point is on a minor road which goes north-east from Llanbedr Dyffryn-Clwyd, over the Bwlch Penbarras pass. It's not the easiest to find unless you have a 1:50,000 Ordnance Survey map! From there, an easy two-kilometre walk along a well-trodden path leads to the top of the hill – a surprisingly gentle walk for a 'wild' feeling peak. The more adventurous could begin an ascent from the village of Cilcain below to the north, although this is a more strenuous route.

Start/parking: Car park at Bwlch Penbarras

Satnav: CH7 5SH (nearest)	**Start GR:** SJ 161605	**High Point GR:** SJ 161626
OS Map: Landranger 116 Denbigh & Colwyn Bay		
Distance: 5km	**Ascent:** 200m	**Time:** 2hrs

Cafe/Pub: In Ruthin, the interesting Ruthin Craft Centre is nearby and has a nice cafe with a contemporary feel. (01824 704774, www.ruthincraftcentre.org.uk).

Directions

Start from the car park at Bwlch Penbarras, which is on a minor road 1.5km NE of Llanbedr-Dyffryn-Clwyd, which is itself 2.5km ENE along the A494 road from Ruthin to Mold. The car park is located where the road crosses Offa's Dyke and is at the crest of the hill.

Follow the well-worn Offa's Dyke path broadly N for 2km up to the summit of Moel Famau. The top is marked by the Jubilee Tower, next to which there is a trig point.

Nearby

Visit St Winefride's Well at Holywell, which has been a pilgrimage site since the seventh century and whose waters are alleged to have miraculous healing powers (www.saintwinefrideswell.com).

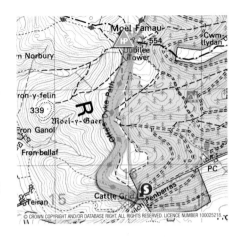

▲ MOEL FAMAU'S SUMMIT, JUBILEE TOWER

▲ LOOKING SOUTH ALONG OFFA'S DYKE PATH

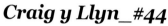

Glamorgan

Craig y Llyn_#44

600m | 1,969ft

66th | 21/05/10 | solo

As the industrial revolution took off, huge natural resources of coal and a convenient coastal location meant that Glamorgan's importance grew dramatically. Demand for coal soared across the UK, and, as some of the largest seams were found in the valleys to the north of the county, Glamorgan thrived. This readily available coal also meant that, with easy access to metal ores, the county soon developed a booming metal industry. Copper, iron and tinplate were produced in massive amounts. At one point, Glamorgan produced over two-thirds of Britain's copper. The towns and cities along the coast swelled as metalworks opened and ports thrived. Glamorgan became a key part of the Industrial Revolution.

Glamorgan is well known for its two major towns, Cardiff and Swansea, which are the largest and third-largest cities in Wales respectively. Both owe their size and dominance to the industrial revolution, when they swelled in size through trading copper and coal. North of the towns are the famous Welsh Valleys. Full of the remnants of the mining industry, employment in the valleys suffered heavily after the collapse of the coal industry. Today, the valleys are a mix of terraced houses and beautiful countryside, but marked by social and economic problems as a result of the industrial decline.

It is in the valleys that you will find the county top, Craig y Llyn. It was not, unfortunately, my favourite high point as the top was buried in a forest and the walk, which began along a heavy trunk road full of heavy lorries and litter and then ran through a scruffy stubble of felled trees, was not the most pleasant. It had an uncomfortable, even spooky or dangerous feel to it and so I was pleased the walk was only forty minutes each way! I saw no one on the walk, other than a couple of mountain bikers on the forest tracks.

Start/parking: Car park on A4061 SW of Hirwaun

Satnav: Hirwaun (nearest)	**Start GR:** SN 927031	**High Point GR:** SN 906031
OS Map: Landranger 170 Vale of Glamorgan West		
Distance: 4km	**Ascent:** 110m	**Time:** 1.5hrs
Cafe/Pub: Try the Angel Inn, Pontneddfechan (01639 722013).		

Directions

Start from the car park at the north-facing viewpoint on the A4061 SW of Hirwaun. The car park is towards the end of a big hairpin bend, just before the road descends down to the Rhonnda valley.

Follow the road W for 0.2km until it turns S. Go W for 0.7km on the track (the Coed Morgannwg Way) from the bend in the road; after crossing open land with impressive views over Llyn Fawr and beyond to the Brecon Beacons, the track goes through recently felled woodland. At a slate signpost standing stone, turn left for 200m down a track to the Craig y Llyn high point. The top is a trig point on raised ground, by the side of the track and next to fir trees. I found the route had a somewhat uncomfortable, even spooky, feel to it!

Nearby

Drive south down the A4061 through the Rhonnda valley. An atmospheric valley, full of the signs of the past coal-mining days. Also, to the west, visit the Gower peninsula, where there are lovely coastal walks.

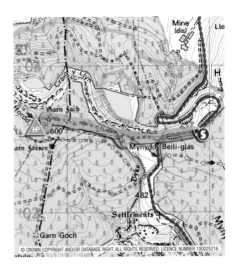

▲ CRAIG Y LLYN SUMMIT

▲ LLYN FAWR BELOW CRAIG Y LLYN

Gloucestershire

Cleeve Cloud_#61

330m | 1,083ft

16ᵗʰ | 06/08/08 | with Harry

Gloucestershire is perhaps best known for the Cotswolds, which stretch across the county as a green swathe countryside. An Area of Outstanding Natural Beauty covered in open fields split by hedgerows, small areas of woodland and gently-rolling hills, they are full of lovely picture-book villages of local yellow Cotswold stone (such as Stow on the Wold, Moreton-in-Marsh, Chipping Camden and Bourton-on-the-Water) and are a particularly pleasant place to spend time.

Gloucestershire is also known for its cheeses. There are two types of Gloucester Cheese – single and double. The single is traditionally made exclusively using the milk from the rare (and once almost extinct) Gloucester cattle while the double, which can be made using milk from other breeds, is the cheese used in the world-famous 'cheese rolling' event in the Cotswolds. A seven-pound cheese is rolled down the incredibly steep Cooper's Hill, whilst people chase after it – the winner being the person who manages to catch the cheese. Needless to say, this isn't the safest event around!

The county top is in the north of the Cotswolds – on Cleeve Common, which overlooks Cheltenham, and is just off the Cotswold Way. The high point is at the side of the Common, next to a field, near to some radio masts. Seemingly unremarkable spots such as this are always strangely interesting, as they illustrate the huge diversity of what you find when visiting Britain's county high points. A seemingly worthier spot would be the 317-metre-high Cleeve Hill, which is nearby and requires a longer walk across the Common to reach. From this point, there are lovely views across to Wales.

Start/parking: Car park at SO 994248

Satnav: GL54 4HA (nearest)   **Start GR:** SO 994248   **High Point GR:** SO 996245

OS Map: Landranger 163 Cheltenham & Cirencester

Distance: 1km   **Ascent:** 0m   **Time:** 0.5hrs

Cafe/Pub: Drop north off Cleeve Hill into Winchcombe for a choice of several pubs and cafes. Alternatively, there are many cafes in nearby Cheltenham.

Directions

Start from the car park by some radio masts at the end of the minor road which goes 5km WNW then N from Whittington. Whittington is 1km NW of the A40 at Andoversford.

Follow the path to the field just past the radio masts, then go SE by a fence along the side of a field for 400m to Cleeve Cloud. The top is a trig point.

Nearby

Visit the lovely regency town of Cheltenham, Tewkesbury Abbey, Sudeley Castle, or the canal boat museum (officially the Gloucester Waterways Museum) in Gloucester docks, where you can explore historic boats, take a canal trip or get wet hands in the interactive canal lock exhibit. www.canalrivertrust.org.uk/gloucester-waterways-museum

▲ HARRY ON TOP OF CLEEVE CLOUD

▲ CLEEVE CLOUD

Pilot Hill_#66

286m | 938ft

9th | 20/06/08 | solo

Hampshire – home to Jane Austen and Charles Dickens, 'birthplace' of the Royal Navy, and the place where cricket was invented (it was in Hambledon in the eighteenth century that one of the earliest teams was formed and the laws of the game formalised).

The county is a large one, stretching from the south coast near Southampton and Portsmouth almost to Reading and the M4. A pleasant county, Hampshire has many green fields and old woodlands and it is one of the few places in the country where wild boar still roam free.

The county top is Pilot Hill, on the North Hampshire Downs in the north of the county. The Downs are a chalk ridge within the North Wessex Downs Area of Outstanding Natural Beauty, the top being open grassland and the lower slopes somewhat wooded. The high point is near to the Wayfarer's Walk – a long distance footpath running across much of southern England. Finding the top is a little tricky, as it is not visible from the Wayfarer's Walk approach route, and precise map reading and time estimation is required. I saw no one on this route, but was pleased to happen upon a deer and many butterflies.

Start/parking: Car park on the E side of Walbury Hill

Satnav: NONE	Start GR: SU 380616	High Point GR: SU 398601
OS Map: Landranger 174 Newbury & Wantage		
Distance: 4.5km	Ascent: 30m	Time: 1.5hrs
Cafe/Pub: There are various cafes in nearby Newbury.		

Directions

Start from the car park on the E side of Walbury Hill. This is on a road 3km SSE from Inkpen to Faccombe.

Follow the Wayfarer's Walk track ESE for 2km, along the sides of fields and woods. 200m after passing some woods on your right, leave the track and head S across a field for 150m to Pilot Hill. The top is a trig point; this cannot be seen from the track, so can be quite tricky to find.

Combine the walk with one to Walbury Hill, the Berkshire high point. The routes have the same starting point. See page 62.

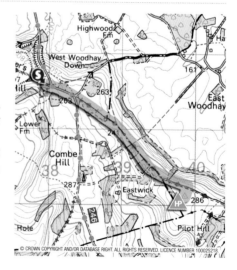

Nearby

Travel south to Winchester Cathedral, which is the longest Gothic cathedral in Europe and over 1,000 years old. Further afield, visit Portsmouth Historic Dockyard, the home of the Royal Navy, where you can see Nelson's HMS Victory, the Mary Rose and HMS Warrior.

▲ THE TRIG POINT ON TOP OF PILOT HILL

Black Mountain_#36

703m | 2,306ft   36th | 18/03/09 | with Harry

I often feel that Herefordshire, right on the border of England and Wales, is quite an underrated county. Its towns are full of timber-framed historic buildings and its countryside full of lush green grass and farming fields, all of which give the county a special feel.

A large proportion of the county is made up of agricultural land, and Herefordshire is famous for its beef and cider. Herefordshire beef cattle are now common across the world, and are so docile and gentle in nature that Hereford United FC use one as their mascot. Apple and pear orchards are prolific in Herefordshire, resulting in a strong tradition of cider-making throughout the county. The region is among the leading cider producers in the UK. See www.ciderroute.co.uk for more.

The county top is Black Mountain – a confusing name, given that it lies in the Black Mountains range and that several mountains and hills around the Welsh borders claim the same name. Our Black Mountain lies exactly on the England/Wales border and is part of the Hatterrall Ridge of hills which divide the two countries.

The route up the Black Mountain is over grassy slopes but towards the top gives way to heathery moorland, which was wonderfully golden at the time of my visit with Harry. We combined Black Mountain with a walk up Chwarel y Fan (Monmouthshire's high point, p162), which is just a few miles away. I imagine there are superb views from Hay Bluff (a point at the west end of the hill, looking out over Wales), but it was in mist when we were there.

Interestingly, Herefordshire has links to other county tops. The lovely River Wye, much beloved by anglers and the fifth-longest river in Britain, winds through the county from its source on the slopes of Plynlimon, the Cardiganshire high point (p82), before returning to Wales. Offa's Dyke path runs over the top of Black Mountain and along the Hatterrall Ridge before heading north to Flintshire, where it crosses another county top, Moel Famau (p120).

Start/parking: Car park at the Gospel Pass
Satnav: NP7 7NP (nearest)   **Start GR:** SO 236350   **High Point GR:** SO 255350
OS Map: Landranger 161 The Black Mountains
Distance: 7km   **Ascent:** 160m   **Time:** 3hrs
Cafe/Pub: Hay-on-Wye (five kilometres north) is undoubtedly the place to go after the walk. Shepherds Ice Cream Parlour & Coffee Bar in Castle Street or Hay Wholefoods & Delicatessen in Lion Street are good options.

Directions

Start from the car park at the Gospel Pass, which is at the top of the minor road from Llanthony to Hay-on-Wye.

Follow the track NE for 1.5km up the grassy slopes and along the top of Ffynnon y Parc, as far as the trig point at Hay Bluff. Then continue on the track SE then SSE for 1.5km along the flat, heathery moorland of Black Mountain. The top is unmarked and is not possible to find precisely as it is so flat.

Nearby

An excellent place to visit is Hereford Cathedral, where you can see the Mappa Mundi (the unique thirteenth-century map of the world), a 1217 version of the Magna Carta (which I hadn't previously known had been revised post 1215) and the unusual Chained Library. www.herefordcathedral.org

Also visit Ross-on-Wye and Ledbury, both of which are pleasant places with independent shops and have an interesting Market House.

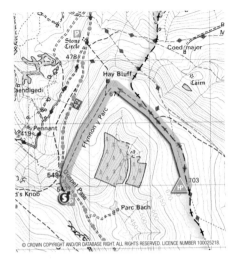

▲ HARRY ON OFFA'S DYKE PATH AT THE BLACK MOUNTAIN SUMMIT POST

▲ ON BLACK MOUNTAIN

Hertfordshire

Pavis Wood_#74

244m | 801ft   12ᵗʰ | 26/06/08 | solo

Lying just north of London, Hertfordshire is one of the Home Counties. With good rail links to the capital, it is a popular home for city commuters looking to escape the hustle and bustle of London. As such, Hertfordshire is a busy county, but, being part of the London green belt, also a green one, full of woodlands and farmed fields.

There are some noteworthy towns in the county, with historic towns rubbing shoulders with more modern settlements. The site of St Albans, for instance, was first settled in the Iron Age and heavily developed by the Romans and, as it was the first stop on the coaching route north from London, later became something of a transport hub. Meanwhile, a few miles away are Letchworth and Welwyn Garden City – two 'new towns' which were, respectively, the first and second 'garden cities' built in the UK. The idea was that these would be towns built within a belt of open countryside, full of open spaces, parks and gardens.

Hertfordshire is one of the few counties (another is Staffordshire) whose high point is not in fact the top of a hill but is instead on the side of it. So Hertfordshire gets bonus points in my book for that! But, despite this distinction, you shouldn't expect too much from Hertfordshire's high point – it is unmarked and in a field a few yards from a road. You have to stop the car and get out to see it, but that's about all. The top in question is Pavis Wood, in rural Hertfordshire near Tring. The summit of the hill upon which the high point lies is actually in Buckinghamshire – whose county top, Haddington Hill, is only a few miles away (see page 70).

Start/parking: Road near Hastoe
Satnav: HASTOE (nearest)   **Start GR:** SP 914092   **High Point GR:** SP 914091 (hilltop)
OS Map: Landranger 165 Aylesbury & Leighton Buzzard
Distance: N/A   **Ascent:** N/A   **Time:** N/A
Cafe/Pub: Available in nearby Tring.

Directions

Start from the road 400m WSW of Hastoe, which is 2km S of Tring, at the point where the road turns to a direction SSE. Pavis Wood is immediately NW of this.

Look E to the high point, which is in the adjacent field. The top is unmarked, in the middle of the field.

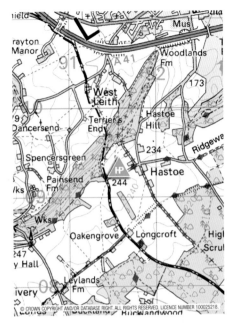

Nearby

Visit St Albans, a small city, historic market town and site of Roman settlements. The abbey (called an abbey although technically it is a cathedral) has the longest nave of any cathedral in England – and there is a good tea spot at Abigail's Tea Rooms in the nearby arcade. Also, visit the remains of the Roman City of Verulamium.

▲ THE HERTFORDSHIRE HIGH POINT

Boring Field_#86

80m | 262ft   33rd | 31/12/08 | with Alex

The historic county of Huntingdonshire lies in the east of England, just north-west of Cambridgeshire, into which it was absorbed in 1974 as part of the 1972 local government reorganisation. As with many other such county restructurings, it lives on with a separate identity in the new county and retains status as a government district – its county town Huntingdon was former Prime Minister John Major's constituency from 1979 to 2001. Interestingly, it was also the constituency and birthplace of Oliver Cromwell, back in the seventeenth century.

Prior to the re-structuring, the county borders of Huntingdonshire had remained virtually unchanged since Saxon times. First settled as far back as the sixth century, the area was invaded by the Danes, who set up Huntingdon as a military centre from which they staged raids into eastern England. The county boundaries were established soon after, and recorded in the Domesday Book, remaining stable until 1974.

The county is quite flat, and close to the marshy fens that lead to the east coast. It is not surprising, then, that Boring Field is (at 262 feet) the lowest of the county high points and is impossible to identify, as the field is so flat. Lying at the intersection of three counties (Huntingdonshire, Bedfordshire and Northamptonshire), the top lies in a very large field, which, at the time I was there (one New Year's Eve), was bare, ploughed earth next to a B road. Boring indeed!

Just south of Peterborough is Holme Fen which, at minus nine feet, is Britain's Low Point (see page 262).

Start/parking: Three Shire Stone on the B645
Satnav: NN9 6BE (nearest)   Start GR: TL 047705   High Point GR: TL 047706
OS Map: Landranger 153 Bedford & Huntingdon
Distance: N/A   Ascent: N/A   Time: N/A
Cafe/Pub: The Buttercups bakery in nearby Kimbolton is a good option for tea and cakes.

Directions

Start from the Three Shire Stone on the verge of the B645, 1km E of Hargrave and 5km ESE of Raunds.

Look N to the high point, which is in the adjacent field. The top is unmarked, in the field.

⬧ BEN NEVIS

BY: ALASDAIR THOMSON

Ben Nevis_#1

1,344m | 4,409ft   5th | Sept. 2006 | with Harry – and Alex for the trip

Inverness-shire is a stunningly beautiful county. Now part of the Highlands Council area, it stretches across Scotland from Inverness to the Outer Hebrides. Inside its borders is a huge swathe of deserted highland: lochs, mountains, moors and forests – some of the most breathtaking countryside in Britain, including Loch Ness, the remote peninsular of Knoydart, the Inner and Outer Hebrides – and Ben Nevis.

Standing at 1,344 metres, Ben Nevis is the highest point of the UK and a huge magnet for visitors. It rises virtually from sea level, meaning that any ascent will be a tough one! (Indeed, the north face is very popular with climbers, offering some of the longest rock climbs in the country.) Due to the popularity of the Ben and the erosion this brings, the walk up is on a wide, stone path, climbing up from the valley to the 'Halfway Lake' at just under 600 metres before heading up the steep and stony slopes above via a zigzagging track. The summit is a barren and rocky plateau, which contains the ruins of a nineteenth-century observatory.

Ben Nevis had major significance for my *High Point* project ambitions as it was success in climbing Ben Nevis which led me to think I could successfully climb other such British peaks. I went up the mountain with Harry. He was sixteen at the time and we made the climb in 2006, four years after he said he wanted to go up Ben Nevis, the attraction to him being that it is Britain's highest point. Happily, our Ben Nevis walk turned out to be a quite straightforward, if a long (ten-hour) day. The route was very popular, the more so as it was the day of the annual Ben Nevis race – the winner got up and down in about 80 minutes, which as I write seems impossible!

Start/parking: Ben Nevis visitor centre

Satnav: PH33 6SX (nearest)   **Start GR:** NN 122729   **High Point GR:** NN 166712

OS Map: Landranger 41 Ben Nevis

Distance: 13km   **Ascent:** 1,330m   **Time:** 10hrs

Cafe/Pub: The Ben Nevis Inn (next to Achintee House) is on the route and a welcome sight at the end of the walk, and the beer is good (01397 701227). Russell's at the Smiddy House in nearby Spean Bridge is a good dinner option. (01397 712335, www.russellsrestaurant.co.uk).

Directions

Start from the car park at the Ben Nevis visitor centre just W of Achintee House. Cross the River Nevis and take the track to Achintee House. There is a clear path on the whole route, except on the summit when it becomes somewhat indistinct. Take the track SE and follow it upwards SE, E then NE for 3km round the steep slopes of Meall an t-Suidhe, until the path forks on the 620m contour near Lochan Meall an t-Suidhe. Head S and follow the path upwards generally ESE for 3.5km to the summit; the path zigzags several times as it rises steadily upwards. The last 500m is across a very rocky, but quite easy to negotiate, summit plateau. The top is a trig point, surrounded by numerous shrines to people's loved ones.

Nearby

Continue south along the valley from the Ben Nevis visitor centre and you'll find the spectacular Steall Falls, Scotland's second largest waterfall. Alternatively, travel the other way, to the sea. Just up from Fort William, at Banavie, is Neptune's Staircase. This is the entrance to the Caledonian Canal and the longest staircase lock in Britain, with eight locks lifting boats by twenty metres.

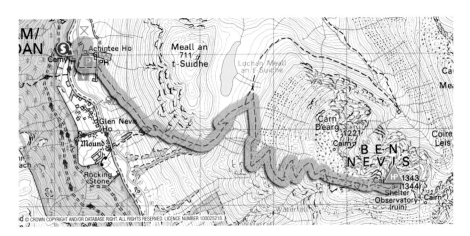

▲ HARRY ON TOP OF BEN NEVIS

▲ ABOVE THE CLOUDS ON BEN NEVIS

Kent

Betsom's Hill_#73

251m | 823ft

20th | 13/08/08 | solo

Think of Kent and images of white cliffs, farmed fields and orchards spring to mind. It's a green county, noted for its crops and agricultural produce and is the warmest county in Britain – a pleasant place to spend time, known as the 'garden of England' for good reason.

The county covers the south-east corner of England, stretching from the Thames to the south coast – where, on a clear day, you can see across the channel to France. It's Britain's oldest county and the one closest to continental Europe. The county has two unexpected county boundaries: one with Essex, set at a defined point in the Thames Estuary, and a ceremonial boundary with France (!) halfway along the Channel Tunnel.

The Kent high point (Betsom's Hill) is, surprisingly, actually inside the M25, just south of Biggin Hill airfield. (There are actually two tops within the motorway, the other being at Bushey Heath in Middlesex – p158.) It sits in the Kent Downs, which are the eastern end of the Surrey Hills – the range containing Surrey's high point, Leith Hill (p226), which is the highest point in south-east England. The precise high point is well-nigh impossible to find as Betsom's Hill is such a flat hilltop and, as there is a lot of private property in the area, the route there is a bit tricky to negotiate. I think I managed to complete the route without trespassing but could not say for sure!

Start/parking: Pilgrims Way minor road
Satnav: TN16 2DT (nearest)   **Start GR:** TQ 432557   High Point GR: TQ 432563
OS Map: Landranger 187 Dorking & Reigate
Distance: 2km   **Ascent:** 80m   Time: 1hr
Cafe/Pub: Available in nearby Westerham.

Directions

Start on the verge of the Pilgrims Way minor road, just N of Gaysham Farm. This can be reached from the A233 at Betsoms Farm, just N of the M25, 1.5km N of Westerham.

Follow the footpath, in many places overgrown, which goes N from Gaysham Farm, up the woody hill and across the North Downs Way for 500m until alongside Little Betsom's Farm. The top is unmarked, somewhere in this flat area.

Nearby

Just south of the M25, visit the historic properties at Chartwell, Knole, Ightham Mote and Hever Castle. Further afield, visit Leeds Castle, Chatham Historic Dockyard and Canterbury Cathedral (which I found to my surprise has a stronger religious feel to it than anywhere else I have been in the UK).

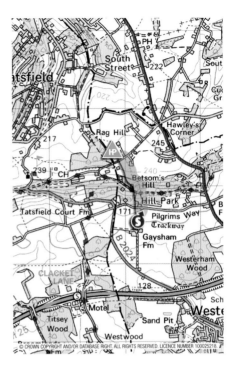

▲ THE FLAT TOP OF BETSOM'S HILL

Mount Battock_#28

778m | 2,552ft   69th | 10/08/10 | solo

Kincardineshire (sometimes called The Mearns) is a county on the east coast of Scotland, just below Aberdeenshire. It ceased to exist in the 1970s – a lot later than the town of Kincardine, after which the county is named, which ceased to exist in the Middle Ages. Luckily, the high point, Mount Battock, still does.

Mount Battock is on Kincardineshire's south-western border with Angus, and I had heard of neither before starting my *High Point* project. At 2,552 feet (778 metres) in height, it is classified as a Corbett – a name given to any Scottish mountain that stands between 2,500 and 3,000 feet high, provided that the summit is 'independent' enough to rise 500 feet above the surrounding ground. Mount Battock is the most easterly Corbett in the country. Its parent peak, Mount Keen, is the most easterly Munro (peaks above 3,000 feet).

I had a worrying walk up Mount Battock. Route finding was tricky at the start, but then became relatively straightforward on a track through heather moorland. However, as I was wandering through thick mist, about twenty minutes' walk from the top of the mountain, I heard thunder rolling up the valley below. And where there's thunder, there's usually lightning ... what to do? Where, or indeed whether, to shelter? This was the first time that I'd encountered thunder and lightning on an exposed hillside. I had heard that the best thing to do is to lie spread-eagled on the ground. However, lying face down in soggy grass and mud while waiting for the storm to cross the valley didn't seem particularly appealing – so I headed back down, fast!

Start/parking: Phone box west of Millden Lodge

Satnav: DD9 7YT (nearest)	Start GR: NO 540789	High Point GR: NO 549844
OS Map: Landranger 44 Ballater & Glen Clova		
Distance: 14km	Ascent: 640m	Time: 6.5hrs

Cafe/Pub: 12 kilometres south-east in Edzell are two good cafes – the Edzell Tweed House and the Tuck Inn.

▲ MOUNT BATTOCK FROM THE SOUTH

Directions

Start from the public phone box just W of Millden Lodge.

Follow the minor road NW for 500m to Mill of Aucheen. Bear NE on the track towards Muir Cottage but, before reaching it, take the track E towards the woods. Follow the track NNE along the W side of the woods to a ford, approx. 1km from the Mill of Aucheen. Continue along the track NNE for 800m until just before a ford over the Burn of Turret.

Do not cross the ford, but instead stay W of the burn and continue up the track in a generally northerly direction for 3.5km until the track is due to fork, soon after some grouse butts. This fork is hard to spot and the track thereafter across Wester Cairn is somewhat indistinct, so care is needed here if in mist. Head NE across Wester Cairn and up to the unusually named (for Scotland) Mount Battock. The top is a trig point.

Nearby

Visit the pleasant small town of Stonehaven, Kincardineshire's county town and originally an Iron Age fishing village.

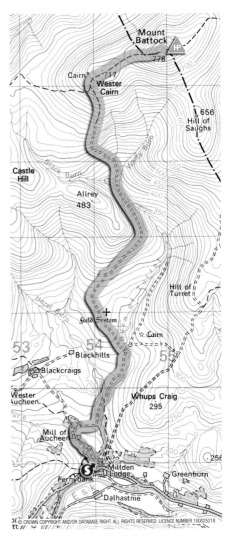

▲ ON TOP OF MOUNT BATTOCK

Kinross-shire

Innerdouny Hill_#56

497m | 1,631ft

62nd | 30/04/10 | solo

Kinross-shire is, after neighbouring Clackmannanshire, the second smallest county in Scotland, with an area of only about fifteen by nine miles – a significant chunk of which is taken up by Loch Leven, a large inland loch and nature reserve. The Loch is just under four miles across at its longest point, but was significantly larger before it was partially drained in the early nineteenth century. During this draining, an ivory and silver sceptre bearing the legend 'Mary Queen of Scots' was found. Mary was imprisoned on an island in the Loch in 1567, escaping a year later and possibly dropping the sceptre in the process.

The county top, Innerdouny Hill, is in the middle of a Forestry Commission forest, just east of the Ochil Hills. It is somewhat tricky to reach as access through the forest was, at the time of my visit, restricted (*No Unauthorised Persons Allowed Beyond This Point* signs) and some savvy was needed to find a route to the top which does not involve picking through the dense forest. Some parts of the forest have been felled and all that is left is unsightly, messy stubble. My trip was a bit nerve-racking as for some reason I always find walking in these kinds of forests somewhat spooky, claustrophobic and threatening. The actual top is marked by a trig point. From there, you can look out over Loch Leven and towards the Lomond Hills.

Start/parking: Littlerig car park on the B934

Satnav: DUNNING (closest)   Start GR: NO 012070   High Point GR: NO 032073

OS Map: Landranger 58 Perth & Alloa

Distance: 6km   Ascent: 200m   Time: 3hrs

Cafe/Pub: Try the Kirkstyle pub just north in Dunning (01764 684248, www.kirkstyle-dunning.co.uk).

▲ LOOKING SOUTH-EAST FROM INNERDOUNY HILL TOWARDS LOCH LEVEN

Directions

Start from the Littlerig car park. This is on the B934, 8km N of splendidly-named Yetts o' Muckhart. The route from here goes through Forestry Commission woodland, and there may be restrictions if the land is being worked.

Follow the track E then NE for 1.3km until the track forks. Take the right fork and follow this largely through cleared forest; after 300m head S through the forest for 200m, until reaching the wall which is marked on the OS 1:25,000 map. The other side of this is a fire break gap through the forest; follow this up for 800m E then ENE until the wall turns through 90 degrees to a SE direction. Continue SE along the wall for 400m until you emerge from the forest. Then head WSW for 200m to the summit of Innerdouny Hill. The top is a trig point.

Nearby

Loch Leven is nearby – visit the nature reserve, or one of the nearby castles. www.visitlochleven.org

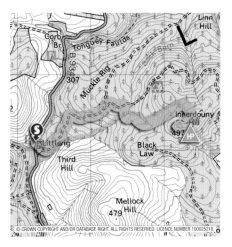

▲ THE SUMMIT OF INNERDOUNY HILL

▲ LOOKING NORTH-WEST FROM INNERDOUNY HILL

Kirkcudbrightshire

Merrick_#17

843m | 2,766ft 63rd | 06/05/10 | solo

Kirkcudbrightshire (it's pronounced *kirr-koo-bree-shar*) was a historic county in the south-west corner of Scotland, on the coast of the Solway Firth. Today part of Dumfries and Galloway, it is a lovely, wide open county and somewhat underrated (or even unknown) by those south of the border.

Fought over by Saxons, Danes and Picts, it was invaded by the English, retaken by the Scots and then squabbled over by various families for years. One name from this history of power-struggles has, however, been remembered above all others – even if he wasn't *quite* involved. This was Mac Bethad mac Findlaích, king of Scotland from 1040 until his death in 1057, and otherwise known as Macbeth and who has been immortalised (inaccurately – there were probably fewer witches and ghosts) in Shakespeare's 'Scottish Play'.

The county top, Merrick, is in the Galloway Forest Park, Britain's first Dark Sky Park. Sadly, it was overcast during my visit, so I couldn't take advantage of the dark skies to see the stars. My route began near the interesting Bruce's Stone, which marks the site of a victory by Robert the Bruce over the English in 1307, and, at the summit, offered views to Ireland and Ailsa Craig. Along the way, I passed the bizarrely-named 'Neive of the Spit' and the 'Rig of the Gloon' – just two of the amazing names in the area: there are also the 'Rhinns of Kells', 'Braes of Mullachgeny', and the 'Lump of the Eglin'. Merrick itself is part of the 'range of the awful hand'. Clearly this is somewhere a bit different!

I had been keen to visit Merrick since university, some forty years ago, when a fellow student had frequently waxed lyrical about the hill. Fortunately, it proved to be everything he claimed and didn't disappoint. A fine day out.

Start/parking: Car park near Bruce's Stone

Satnav: DG8 6SY (the visitor centre)	**Start GR:** NX 413802	**High Point GR:** NX 427855
OS Map: Landranger 77 Dalmellington & New Galloway		
Distance: 12km	**Ascent:** 760m	**Time:** 6.5hrs

Cafe/Pub: Glentrool visitor centre, five kilometres south-west, is a good spot for a cup of tea, as is the Smithy Tearoom in nearby New Galloway.

Directions

Start from the car park near Bruce's Stone on the N side of Loch Trool. This is at the E end of the minor road which joins the A714 10km NW of Newton Stewart.

Follow the track N for nearly 2km along the W side of Buchan Burn; most of the second part of this is alongside or through woods. At Culsharg the path turns NW; follow this, but after 300m note the path has a dog-leg right and then left when it reaches a forest track. 1.5km from Culsharg, having exited the wood and the path turned N, the path reaches a stone wall 500m SW of Benyellary. Follow the wall NE to the cairn at the top of Benyellary. Follow the path N and then NE along the Neive of the Spit for 2km to the Merrick. The top is a trig point.

Nearby

A short stroll from the car park is the Bruce's Stone, from where there is a superb viewpoint over Glen Trool. Also nearby is the interesting, picturesque little town of Kirkcudbright, which is noted for its artists' quarter.

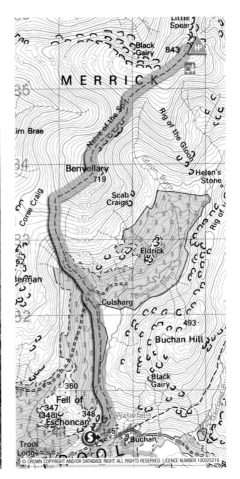

▲ MERRICK FROM THE TOP OF BENYELLARY

▲ BENYELLARY, THE NEIVE OF THE SPIT AND MERRICK FROM THE SOUTH

Culter Fell_#31

748m | 2,454ft   76th | 07/10/10 | solo

Lying between the cities of Glasgow and Edinburgh, it shouldn't be surprising to discover that the former county of Lanarkshire is (or rather *was*, as it is yet another of those counties removed in the 1970s) one of the most populous areas of Scotland. Upon its demise, the council became part of the Strathclyde region, although this was itself then divided further. Now, the area of old Lanarkshire is roughly split between the counties of New and Old Lanarkshire.

The county top, Culter Fell, now lies in South Lanarkshire and is the high point of that county. The top is part of the Southern Uplands, a term used to describe several ranges of hills which lie in southern Scotland. Among these ranges are the Cheviots (containing Cheviot – Northumberland's county top, p176), the Lammermuirs (Meikle Says Law – Berwickshire, p64) and the Galloway Hills (Merrick – Kirkcudbrightshire, p142).

Culter Fell itself sits between the rivers Clyde and Tweed, near the town of Biggar. Covered in heather moorland, which sits in stark contrast to the green surroundings, the view from the top can stretch from the Lake District to the Highlands. Before I arrived in Lanarkshire, I had thought my visit would be nothing special, but it turned out the walk, the delightful B&B I stayed in (www.cormistonfarm.com) and the local village (Biggar) far exceeded my expectations – a pleasant surprise.

Start/parking: Road verge near Birthwood

Satnav: ML12 6QB	**Start GR:** NT 030311	**High Point GR:** NT 052290
OS Map: Landranger 72 Upper Clyde Valley		
Distance: 6km	**Ascent:** 490m	**Time:** 4hrs
Cafe/Pub: The Aroma cafe in nearby Biggar has tasty tea and cakes (01899 220009).		

Directions

Start from the W verge, 300m NE of Birthwood and just past the turn to Culter Allers Farm, on the minor road from Coulter to Coulter Reservoir.

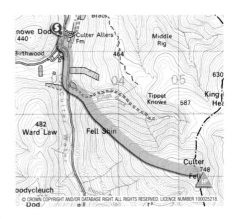

Follow the road S towards Coulter Reservoir. (**Note:** there are signs which assert that the number of walkers in one group should not exceed four.) 800m from the start, take the track SE which goes along Kings Beck. Leave it after 200m and follow SSE, then SE, the crown of the hill past some grouse butts and up Fell Shin. Continue upwards on this track – this levels out soon after the cairn marked on the map and then all but disappears as the ground becomes quite boggy. Continue ESE, the ground soon becoming firmer, up to Culter Fell. The top is a trig point.

▲ CULTER FELL'S SUMMIT

Nearby

The Falls of Clyde at New Lanark are an impressive sight and today are a Site of Special Scientific Interest. The Falls were harnessed by the New Lanark cotton mills, which depended on the power generated by the water. The mills, which used water-powered cotton spinning machinery invented by Richard Arkwright, were at the heart of the Industrial Revolution and became famous as a model industrial community under the enlightened management of Robert Owen in the early nineteenth century. Now impeccably restored, they are a UNESCO World Heritage Site and well worth a visit. www.newlanark.org

▲ LOOKING NORTH-WEST FROM FELL SHIN TOWARDS TINTO

Lancashire (old definition)

Old Man of Coniston_#24

803m | 2,634ft   87th | 11/04/12 | with Tim and Anne

Lancashire's high point is a confusing one. Historically, the county, established in the twelfth century, ran from Liverpool into the Lake District. The modern-day county is smaller – having lost land to the south and, crucially, the north. This lost land reached well into the south Lakes, and included the Old Man of Coniston: the county top – now part of Cumbria.

Today's Lancashire, then, must have a different top – which is again tricky to pin down. There are two candidates: Gragareth, 627 metres high and 200 metres within the county boundary, and Green Hill, a metre higher and right on the border. Both have supporters and both appear on different county top lists. To be on the safe side, I visited all three tops, walking over Green Hill and Gragareth on the same day I visited one of Yorkshire's equally-disputed high points, Whernside (see page 257), and climbing the Old Man four years later. I approached the latter walk with foreboding as it was my first high point since my broken leg seven months previously. I was glad to be accompanied by my brother Tim and his wife Anne; in the event, all was well, quite a relief! Luckily, the route is straightforward, albeit steep, and at the top we were treated to superb views across the Lakeland peaks and Morecombe Bay.

The Old Man of Coniston lies in the northernmost part of Old Lancashire, near the village of Coniston. Although only the twenty-ninth highest peak in the Lake District, the Old Man is popular with walkers. It is a rather attractive, craggy mountain, towering above the village and looking down on Coniston Water below – famous as the scene of Donald Campbell's world water speed records in Bluebird some fifty years ago. The only man to hold both land and water speed records at the same time, he died on the lake during an attempt in which he was travelling at over 300 miles per hour.

Start/parking: Information Centre, Coniston

Satnav: LA21 8EH   **Start GR:** SD 303975   **High Point GR:** SD 272978

OS Map: Landranger 90 Penrith & Keswick

Distance: 6km   **Ascent:** 750m   **Time:** 5km

Cafe/Pub: In Coniston, the Bluebird cafe (by the steamboats pier, 015394 41649, www.thebluebirdcafe.co.uk) is a good spot for tea, as is the cafe at the interesting Brantwood House across Coniston Water.

Directions

Start next to the Information Centre in Coniston. This is on the B5285, 200m E of the A593.

Follow the B5285 up to the bridge where the A593 crosses Church Beck and take the minor road NW, passing the Sun Inn after 200m from the bridge. This road becomes a footpath 200m after the Sun Inn. Follow the path NW along the W side of Church Beck for 400m to Miners Bridge (do not cross this) and then continue along it some 2.5km up to the summit – the path initially goes NW and then W before turning SW and W in the final steep ascent to the top. The middle third of this 2.5km stretch is through disused slate mines. The top is a big cairn, which is next to a trig point.

An alternative route (10km in total) is to start the walk at the Three Shire Stone on Wrynose Pass. From there a path goes SW up to Little Carrs and then S along a broad ridge to Great Carrs, Swirl How, Brim Fell and the Old Man of Coniston.

Nearby

Across Coniston Water is Brantwood House: '*the most beautifully situated house in the Lake District*', where the important thinker and critic John Ruskin lived for many years in the nineteenth century. When we visited, we came across one of those splendidly eccentric British moments – new public toilets being formally opened to music from a local brass band, its members all decked out in their best red tunics, followed by speeches from local dignitaries, all recorded by the local media, and all this looking out at what must be one of the best views in Britain (across Coniston Water to the Old Man et al). A truly magical moment! www.brantwood.org.uk

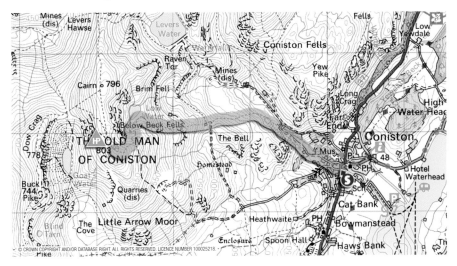

Leicestershire

Bardon Hill_#69

278m | 912ft   21ˢᵗ | 21/08/08 | solo

Never mind county tops – Lindley Hall Farm, near Fenny Drayton in Leicestershire, is the most central point in England. Of course, as is always the case with such things, this is disputed. A point in Warwickshire claims the title, as it is the furthest point from the sea, and the 'Midland Oak' in the same county marks the spot midway along the north–south and east–west lines of the country. Lindley Hall Farm, however, is the Ordnance Survey's official 'centroid' point (the point on which the country, if it were cut out, would balance) and bears a plaque to say as much.

Leicestershire – as should be apparent from the paragraph above – lies in the Midlands. It's a county noted in several different and contrasting ways. Much of the county is industrial. It is recognised as a centre of engineering and, as might be obvious from the town of Coalville, has a strong mining history. Elsewhere, however, the county is heavily rural, and is known for its scenery and, in the past, for its fox-hunting traditions.

On a similar note, the last wild bear in England was allegedly killed at the county top, Bardon Hill. Standing only 278 metres tall, the hill isn't particular large, but, thanks to the county's flat landscape, is visible from a considerable distance. It was an odd place to visit, as the top is perched immediately above the edge of the large Bardon Quarry, which has hacked away a significant proportion of the west face of the hill (the east side is a protected Site of Special Scientific Interest). Surprisingly, the hill is actually an extinct volcano, sitting on an ancient faultline which stretches from Derbyshire to Germany. It is pink granite created by this volcano that is quarried on the hill.

Start/parking: Greenhill Road, Coalville

Satnav: LE67 4UF	**Start GR:** SK 457142	**High Point GR:** SK 459131
OS Map: Landranger 129 Nottingham & Loughborough		
Distance: 2.5km	**Ascent:** 60m	**Time:** 1.5hrs

Cafe/Pub: There's plenty of choice in nearby (and splendidly named) Ashby de la Zouch.

Directions

Start from Greenhill Road, on the eastern outskirts of Coalville. This can be easily accessed from junction 22 on the M1.

Find the Ivanhoe Way 200m W of the 232m spot point at Agar Nook Lane, and follow it for 200m SSE through a housing estate until you reach open ground. Follow it 500m SSE across fields until the track reaches a wood. Go ENE for 200m along the side of the wood, and then head SSE along a path into the woods. After 500m the path turns W and goes to the top of Bardon Hill. The top is a trig point, from where there is a surprising and interesting view over Bardon Quarry.

Nearby

Visit Melton Mowbray, which is famous for its pork pies and Stilton cheese. There is a regular farmers' market selling local produce every Tuesday.

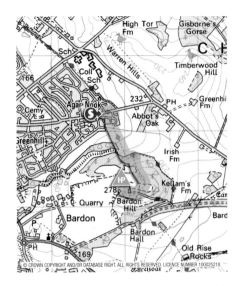

▲ BARDON HILL SUMMIT

▲ BARDON QUARRY FROM BARDON HILL

Normanby Top_#80

168m | 551ft   15th | 23/07/08 | with Alex

Lincolnshire is big – the second largest county in England. It covers a significant proportion of the east coast, starting near the top of Norfolk and running up to the River Humber. As with much of the east coast, it's a very flat county, containing much of the Fens, a large area of naturally marshy land. Now drained, they support a high level of agriculture – as does Lincolnshire as a whole. The flat nature of Lincolnshire gives it, in some circles, a reputation for being rather dull, but I must say I found its wide open spaces quite appealing.

Surprisingly for such a flat county, Lincolnshire contains the highest area of land in eastern England between Yorkshire and Kent – the Lincolnshire Wolds. Designated an Area of Outstanding Natural Beauty, they are a small range of low-lying chalk hills and open valleys that run roughly parallel with the coast. It is here that you'll find the high point: Normanby Top.

Normanby Top – sometimes called the Wolds Top – is in the north of the county, just south-west of Grimsby, in a huge corn field near a distinctive radio mast. The top is on a large plateau and is marked on the map as a trig point, but we were unable to spot it amongst the extensive hedgerows and corn fields. It is presumably there somewhere, but we left without finding it as we were not on a footpath and did not want to overstay our welcome in the fields.

The highlight of my trip to Lincolnshire was seeing the Boston Stump, St Botolph's Church in Boston, which has a jaw-droppingly high tower (272 feet) which is astonishing and can be seen across the Fenlands for miles. Grimsby also has an eye-opening tower, the 309-feet-high Grimsby Dock Tower, which provides hydraulic power to the locks and cranes of Grimsby Docks.

Start/parking: Radar station NE of Normanby le Wold

Satnav: LN7 6SS (nearest)	**Start GR:** TF 124961	**High Point GR:** TF 121964
OS Map: Landranger 113 Grimsby		
Distance: 2km	**Ascent:** 0m	**Time:** 1hrs

Cafe/Pub: There's nothing particularly close by, unfortunately, so head for Steel's Cornerhouse restaurant (rightly renowned locally for its fish & chips) in Cleethorpes (01472 692644, www.steelscornerhouse.co.uk).

Directions

Start from the radar station on the minor road 1km NE of Normanby le Wold.

Follow the side of the field NW for 400m. The high point is in this flat area. The top is marked as a trig point on the map, but I was unable to find it.

Nearby

Visit the Boston Stump and the Grimsby Dock Tower (see opposite). Also, visit the Fenlands to the south – they are a place like no other in Britain, exceptionally flat with rich soil and a remote other-worldly feel. My wife has ancestors from Holbeach and Spalding, so it was interesting to visit there, particularly the Moulton Windmill in Holbeach, which, at 100 feet high, is Britain's tallest.

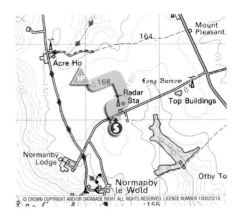

▲LOOKING NORTH FROM NORMANBY TOP

▲ THE GOLDEN FIELDS AROUND NORMANBY TOP

Aran Fawddwy_#14

905m | 2,969ft   89th | 15/08/12 | with Harry and Lou

Merionethshire (*Meirionnydd*) is a large county in north Wales. It covers southern Snowdonia and features a long section of the Welsh coastline at the top of Cardigan Bay – yet, despite its size, it is one of the least densely populated counties in the UK. It is a beautiful and compelling county in which high mountains and wild countryside sit in opposition to the huge open cast slate mines that have dominated the region's history.

The county top is Aran Fawddwy, which, at 905 metres tall, is the sixteenth-highest peak in Wales. It is a beautiful, craggy peak, and a walk up it is a delightful, but straightforward one, with lovely colours and grassy slopes lower down in the Hengwm valley giving way to more barren, rocky features towards the summit. It is little-visited mountain (there were just three other groups on the mountain when we went) in comparison to the more popular peaks further north in Snowdonia, and the nearby Cadair Idris, but for me, this only adds to its appeal.

The peak was a special one for me: this was the last walk on my *High Point* project, and I approached the walk with mixed emotions. I was obviously excited at the prospect of completing my project, but also sad that my four year quest was about to end. I was also somewhat anxious as the walk seemed quite a demanding one, especially as I had not fully recovered my fitness after breaking my leg a year previously. I was accompanied on the walk by my son Harry and his friend Lou. Adverse weather conditions threatened all day, but fortunately did not hit us and at the top we were buzzed by three RAF Tornado fighters. We stayed in nearby Dolgellau, which we found to be a lovely little town and where the restaurant (Y Meirionydd) we ate at after the walk served excellent champagne to help us celebrate the completion of my quest.

Start/parking: Cwm Cywarch car park

Satnav: SY20 9JG (nearest)	Start GR: SH 852187	High Point GR: SH 862223

OS Map: Landranger 124 Porthmadog & Dolgellau

Distance: 11km	Ascent: 760m	Time: 6.5hrs

Cafe/Pub: Don't miss the superb, characterful T.H. Roberts cafe in Dolgellau, which serves excellent tea and cakes (01341 423552).

Directions

Start from the car park at the head of Cwm Cywarch, on the W side of the singletrack road 4km N of Dinas Mawddwy. It is 300m S of Blaencywarch, just N of the unfenced part of the road at Fawnog Fawr.

Follow the road S (right) from the car park for 100m to the footpath signposted *Aran Fawddwy* and *Aran Benllyn*. Follow the path NE – initially this goes through farmland alongside walls and fences until, after 300m, it emerges to open land. The path rises NE steadily for 2km up to the 571m spot point at the col between Waun Goch and Drysgol. There are two short wooden posts to mark this point. Head NNW and follow the W side of the fence for 1km up the grassy slopes to Drysgol, then go W for 1km along the ridge to the cairn which marks the spot where an RAF person was struck by lightning. This looks a very exposed spot on the map but is actually fine to walk on. Then head NW then NNW 700m along the fence until it meets the fence coming up from the SW, and go NE along the fence for the final 500m to the summit. The top is a trig point. You cannot see Aran Fawddwy until you reach Drysgol.

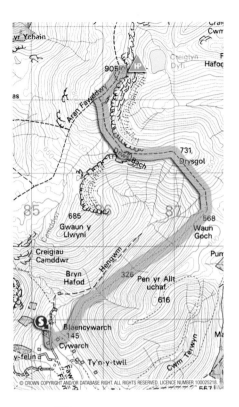

Nearby

Visit the Llechwedd slate caverns in Blaenau Ffestiniog (www.llechwedd-slate-caverns.co.uk), the beach at Barmouth (which we could barely stand up on due to a gale when we visited!) or Harlech Castle – all are good spots.

▲ ARAN FAWDDWY FROM ABOVE DRWS BACH

▲ LOOKING DOWN HENGWM FROM WAUN GOCH

Bushey Heath_#81

155m | 509ft   38th | 22/04/09 | solo

After Rutland, Middlesex is the second smallest county in England, but one that punches well above its weight. The most densely-populated county in Britain, it includes large parts of London (and is virtually entirely made up of urbanised land). It covers roughly the north-west corner of the capital, starting at the Thames and stretching up towards Hertfordshire and Buckinghamshire (very roughly to the M25). Inside its boundaries are the Houses of Parliament and Westminster Abbey – major British institutions! However, the neighbouring City of London, a county in its own right from the twelfth century, harbours the majority of the city's financial establishments, and thus exerts a significant degree of political control over Middlesex.

The county no longer exists, swallowed up by Greater London but, as with so many such counties, its name lives on, perhaps most famously in Middlesex County Cricket Club, whose home ground is Lord's, one of the most famous cricket grounds in the world.

The county top is at Bushey Heath – the highest point in London north of the River. Bushey Heath itself is a small town and is actually now in Hertfordshire. The high point is rather odd – it is the bank of the privately held Three Valleys Water reservoir, which is in a built up area. To see it you have to peek over the walls which surround the reservoir complex. Very unusual!

Start/parking: Intersection of Clay Lane and Windmill Lane

Satnav: WD23 1NW	**Start GR:** TQ 152943	**High Point GR:** TQ 152942
OS Map: Landranger 176 West London		
Distance: 0.3km	**Ascent:** 0m	**Time:** 0.5hrs

Cafe/Pub: The Kanteen bakery and patisserie in Bushey is a good option for tea and cakes (020 8950 0400, www.thekanteen.com).

Directions

Start from Clay Lane – just NW of its intersection with the A409 in Bushey Heath.

Follow Windmill Lane, which intersects with Clay Lane, for 300m and peek over the wall on the left side of the road. The Middlesex high point is the bank of the Three Valleys Water reservoir in front of you.

Nearby

Visit London – truly another country, a different world from the rest of Britain. There are several train stations close to Bushey and nearby Edgware is on the Northern Line if you want to jump on the Tube.

▲ MIDDLESEX'S HIGH POINT

Blackhope Scar_#41

651m | 2,136ft   61st | 29/04/10 | solo

Midlothian is a small county on the southern coast of the Firth of Forth. A short trip away from Edinburgh, it is a quiet region that stretches down across beautiful countryside towards the Scottish borders. This countryside includes the Moorfoot Hills, one of several ranges of hills which collectively make up the Southern Uplands, ranges which contain several county tops. It's a lovely area, with rolling hills, lovely colours and a hint throughout of Edinburgh's class and money. The Moorfoot Hills themselves are designated a Special Area of Conservation thanks to the European Dry Heath and the blanket bogs which are widespread throughout the region, which are drier and thus distinct from those found in other areas of Scotland.

The highest point in the Moorfoot Hills is the delightfully-named Windlestraw Law. That hill, however, lies over the Midlothian county boundary, in Peebles-shire, meaning that Blackhope Scar, eight metres lower, is our high point. The top is a peaty area and is reached via a very pleasant walk alongside Blackhope Water (a small river). On my visit, this was particularly peaceful in the lovely fresh spring air and totally quiet, except for the birds.

Midlothian is associated in my mind with the 1880 Midlothian campaign of the political giant William Gladstone; this is often cited as the first modern political campaign, with his meetings often attended by several thousand people. In his career, Gladstone served as Prime Minister no less than four times, and similarly as Chancellor of the Exchequer.

Start/parking: Windy Slack on the B7007

Satnav: EH38 5YE (nearest)	**Start GR:** NT 350521	**High Point GR:** NT 315483
OS Map: Landranger 73 Peebles, Galashiels & Selkirk		
Distance: 9km	**Ascent:** 430m	**Time:** 4.5hrs

Cafe/Pub: Peebles and Innerleithen, both about fifteen kilometres south, have a number of cafes.

Directions

Start by **Windy Slack** on the B7007, 15km N of Innerleithen.

Follow the track from just N of Windy Slack to Blackhope and along Blackhope Water. Continue to the end of the bridleway, 2km SW of Blackhope. Just past Wooly Burn, cross over the stream and go up the hill which is between Blackhope Water and Rough Burn. Head SW upwards for 1.5km up to the summit of Blackhope Scar. The top is a trig point, with good views over the Moorfoot Hills.

Nearby

Visit Edinburgh, a superb city with wonderful buildings and architecture in both New and Old Towns, a culture quite different from that in the rest of Scotland, interesting places to visit, and with the breadth of activities and talent characteristic of capital cities. The wonderful castle and Arthur's Seat (a striking 251-metre hill rising above the heart of Edinburgh) provide a unique, special backdrop to the city. The flavour of Edinburgh is wonderfully captured in the 2010 film *The Illusionist* which is set in the 1950s. Its weather is also surprisingly good – drier than the Scottish norm.

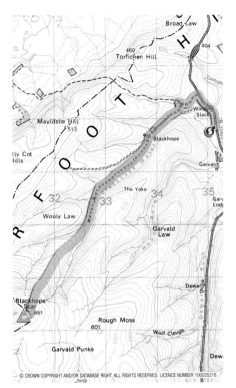

▲ THE TOP OF BLACKHOPE SCAR

▲ THE MOORFOOT HILLS FROM BLACKHOPE SCAR

Chwarel y Fan_#38

679m | 2,228ft   35th | 18/03/09 | with Harry and Joe

Cross the Severn Bridge from England and you're in Monmouthshire – the most south-easterly county in Wales. Although much of the county's eastern boundary consists of the Severn Estuary, it also borders England, and there was, in the past, some dispute over which country the county actually lay in.

   The confusion stemmed from the creation of the county. In the sixteenth century, an Act of Parliament brought Wales under English law, creating Monmouthshire (in Wales) in the process. But a second act put Monmouthshire in England, where it stayed until the twentieth century, despite many of its inhabitants speaking Welsh. This caused no end of confusion and argument: Wales was frequently referred to as 'Wales and Monmouthshire'; some Monmouthshire inhabitants felt English, others Welsh; and, when a sign in Monmouth was erected which read *Welcome to Wales and Monmouthshire*, it was quickly defaced to read *Welcome to Wales*, and then again, to *Welcome*. Luckily, the 1972 Act settled the matter, making Monmouthshire officially Welsh. Perhaps, however, the county motto says it best: *Utrique Fedelis* – 'Faithful to Both'.

   Chwarel y Fan is in Wales's Black Mountains, a range of hills which also claims the distinction of Herefordshire's county top – the confusingly-named Black Mountain, just a few miles away (p128). The summit lies on a narrow, blunt and peaty ridge which stretches southwards from Waun Fach, the 811-metre high point of the Black Mountains. It is marked by a cairn, and offers good views from its steep flanks dropping into the valleys on either side.

   I visited it on a lovely spring day with Harry, Joe Cartwright and his dog Bertie. We started at Llanthony in the pretty Vale of Ewyas, and the trip was very pleasant in the sunshine. The Vale of Ewyas is very secluded and quiet, with only a singletrack road through it – which is quite narrow in places, making the route to the walk's start a little tricky!

Start/parking: Car park at Llanthony

Satnav: NP7 7NN	**Start GR:** SO 289278	**High Point GR:** SO 258294
OS Map: Landranger 161 The Black Mountains		
Distance: 9km	**Ascent:** 460m	**Time:** 4.5hrs

Cafe/Pub: There are two pubs in Llanthony – the Half Moon Inn (01873 890611) and the Llanthony Priory Hotel (01873 890487).

Directions

Start from the car park at Llanthony, in the Vale of Ewyas. To reach this, take the A465 N from Abergavenny; 7km N at Llanvihangel Crucorney, take the left turn to Stanton. Llanthony is approx. 6km NNW from Stanton.

Cross the footbridge over Afon Honddu and take the path W. Follow this for 2km SW up Cwm-bwchel, and past Bal-bach to the cairn at the col. Take the path NW for 500m up Bal-Mawr. Then walk along the ridge for 2.5km past Bwlch Isaf and Bwlch Bach up to Chwarel y Fan. The woods shown on the map at Chwarel y Fan have long gone and only tree stumps remain. The top is a cairn.

Nearby

Next to the car park is the interesting Llanthony Priory – a magnificent ruined abbey, built around the year 1100 AD and which fell into disrepair in the fifteenth century. Entrance is free. Also visit the nearby book town of Hay-on-Wye, and the county town, Monmouth, which has many independent shops and a pleasant feel.

▲ LOOKING NORTH-WEST INTO THE HAZE FROM CHWAREL Y FAN

Moel Sych_ #21

827m | 2,713ft   49th | 05/08/09 | with Joe

Nowadays swallowed by Powys – a gigantic county which runs more than half the length of Wales – the historic Welsh county of Montgomeryshire covers a beautiful and mountainous area of land and reaches across Wales from Shropshire to Machnylleth, near the coast with the Irish Sea.

The county town is Montgomery, a town established around a thirteenth-century Norman castle about a mile from the border with England. A historic market town, it has several interesting old timber-framed houses, cobbled streets and Georgian buildings.

Close by is Offa's Dyke, an earthwork which runs close to (but does not follow) the England/Wales border from Prestatyn on the north Wales coast to near Chepstow on the south coast. It is generally thought to be a boundary between the Anglian kingdom of Mercia and the Welsh kingdom of Powys and was built in the time of Offa, King of Mercia in the eighth century. The dyke is now a long distance path running some 280 kilometres.

Moel Sych is a slightly unfortunate peak in many ways. It was originally thought to be the highest point of the Cadair Berwyn summit ridge. It was then discovered that the most northerly point of the ridge – Cadair Berwyn 'North Top', was of equal height. Then it was discovered that the peak in between the two – Cadair Berwyn 'New Top' – was three metres higher still. Moel Sych was demoted from the highest point in the Berwyn range to joint second. Still, it remains the high point of Montgomeryshire.

The walk to the top is short but sharp, leaving the car park near the impressive Pistyll Rhaeadr falls and climbing steeply up and out on to open, grassy ground. The Berwyn Mountains are a barren and wild place once you are up high, but all the more beautiful for it. A pleasant horseshoe route is possible from the summit, continuing over Cadair Berwyn (the Denbighshire high point) and then dropping eastwards back around Llyn Lluncaws and down, alongside the stream, to the road.

Start/parking: Pistyll Rhaeadr car park

Satnav: SY10 0BZ	Start GR: SJ 075294	High Point GR: SJ 066318
OS Map: Landranger 125 Bala & Lake Vyrnwy		
Distance: 5km	Ascent: 530m	Time: 3.5hrs
Cafe/Pub: Tan-y-Pistyll Cafe, Pistyll Rhaeadr (01691 780392, www.pistyllrhaeadr.co.uk).		

Directions

See the Denbighshire high point (page 96) for full route directions and map.

Nearby

As with the Cadair Berwyn Denbighshire walk, the start is right by the Pistyll Rhaeadr falls.

▲ PISTYLL RHAEADR, THE TALLEST FALLS IN WALES

Morayshire

Carn a Ghille Chearr_#34

710m | 2,329ft   77ᵗʰ | 19/10/10 | solo

Moray is whisky country. There are over fifty distilleries in the area, including many of Scottish whisky's biggest names – Glenlivet, Glenfiddich, Macallan and Aberlour. (The former two are the biggest-selling single malts in the world!) It's hard to pin down the exact reason for this proliferation, although some suggest it is that Speyside has everything the whisky maker could want – fertile land for barley, burns and rivers running with clear water and a perfect climate for the maturation of whisky.

The county lies towards the north-east of Scotland, just below the Moray Firth, and reaches down towards the top of the Cairngorm mountain range – which is where you'll find the county top, Carn a Ghille Chearr, in the Cromdale Hills. These are a line of mainly rounded and broad-topped hills, largely covered in grouse moorland (I came across countless grouse, and a mountain hare) with the added benefit of being near the Glenlivet Distillery.

When I set out to climb Carn a Ghille Chearr, the tops were blanketed by thick cloud, and, as I climbed into the misty air, I got an object lesson in the difficulties of navigation in tricky conditions. It soon started to snow – just a couple of inches but enough to cause an unsettling white-out. There was no footpath, but, as my route seemed straightforward, I pressed on. However, as I walked, the snow settled ... Returning from the summit, I had little choice but to walk into the cloud along a compass bearing, aiming to retrace my steps. Unfortunately, this took me along a wide, convex ridge with no distinguishing features. After fifteen minutes, I was surprised to come across four cairns, which I had not seen on the way up. Nor were they on the map. I was even more surprised fifteen minutes later to find myself back at the top. I had gone full circle and not realised it! In view of the conditions I decided to drop below cloud level as soon as possible and so headed straight downhill on a bearing – to visibility, safety and a slightly longer walk home.

Notwithstanding the trials and tribulations of the walk, there was a lovely bonus later as, when I emerged from the clouds, the sun glinted through the mist down below in Strathavon in a truly special way, changing from moment to moment.

Start/parking: Ballcorach car park

Satnav: AB37 9HP	**Start GR:** NJ 154265	**High Point GR:** NJ 139298
OS Map: Landranger 36 Grantown & Aviemore		
Distance: 10km	**Ascent:** 480m	**Time:** 5hrs

Cafe/Pub: There's the cafe in the Glenlivet distillery a short distance away. See opposite for details. Tip: for the best breakfast scrambled eggs with smoked salmon, stay at the Dunallan House B&B in Grantown on Spey (www.dunallan.com).

Directions

Start from the Ballcorach car park on the B9136 1km north of the Tomintoul distillery.

Follow the track north along the River Avon and round up to the derelict Knock farm. Go through the farm and past a pond, and continue across the grouse moor until the track comes to an end 3km further on. Head NW 400m up to the crown of the ridge, then NE to Carn Eachie, and then N to Carn a Ghille Chearr – there are vehicle tracks intermittently along this route. The top is a trig point.

Nearby

Visit the Glenlivet distillery – about five kilometres north-east – which has a good cafe in its excellent visitor centre (opened in 2010) – www.theglenlivet.com

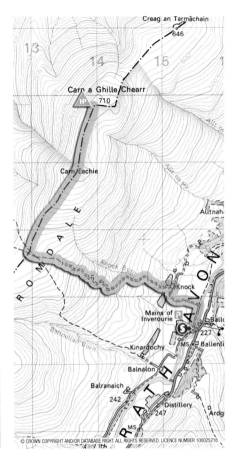

▲ THE TOP OF CARN A GHILLE CHEARR, ACTUALLY IN MIST UNKNOWN TO THE CAMERA

▲ LOOKING NORTH-EAST AFTER EMERGING BELOW THE CLOUDS ON CARN A GHILLE CHEARR

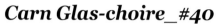

Nairnshire

Carn Glas-choire_#40
659m | 2,162ft   78th | 20/10/10 | solo

Nairnshire began life as a rather 'untidy' county, with a number of exclaves in surrounding counties. In 1891, the Local Government (Scotland) Act – which established elected county councils in Scotland, as they were in England and Wales – merged these exclaves with their host counties, and Nairnshire became a single entity. Nowadays, it is part of the sprawling Highland region.

The county sat in the north of Scotland, between Moray and Inverness on the Moray Firth. It covered a small area of hilly land with what few towns there were located on the coast. These included the county town of Nairn, an ancient fishing port. Over the years, Nairn has been used for training troops prior to the WWII Normandy landings, hosted international golf competitions and grown into a popular seaside resort – apparently it was an annual holiday destination for Charlie Chaplin!

The county top is Carn Glas-choire, which is the highest point on a remote grouse moor on the northern edge of the Cairngorms National Park. The summit, I imagine, is one of those which is only visited by 'baggers' of one sort or another, in my case county high points, in others perhaps Grahams (hills with a height between 2,000 and 2,499 feet) or Marilyns (hills with a relative height of 150 metres, regardless of actual height). The summit is a relatively large plateau of open moorland, which, being fairly wet and mossy, has been described by some as 'dreary'. But given the beauty of the Scottish Highlands generally, it's still a rather pleasant hill to visit. When I was there in the autumn, the trees were golden in the sunshine – I wish I could have bottled the colours. The weather was pleasant and the views lovely right up to the summit: from the top the view was clear as a bell right across to the Cairngorm mountains in the distance. And just me and a mountain hare to witness it. However, the weather changed and a blizzard blew in from the north – typical!

Start/parking: Roadside on B9007

Satnav: PH23 3NB   **Start GR:** NH 930270   **High Point GR:** NH 891291

OS Map: Landranger 35 Kinguissie & Monadhliath Mountains; Landranger 36 Grantown & Aviemore

Distance: 11km   **Ascent:** 370m   **Time:** 4.5hrs

Cafe/Pub: The Old Bakery coffee shop in nearby Carrbridge is a good option (01479 841320).

Directions

Start from the east verge of the B9007 some 750m north of the entrance to the track which goes to Auchterteang.

Follow the road back to the entrance to the track which goes to Auchterteang. Take the track to Auchterteang, and cross your fingers that the dogs at the farm are in their kennels! Continue along the track over the grouse moor for 4km past the Garrocher burn and a green hut until the track finishes near the head of the Allt Glas-choire burn. Head WSW for 500m over boggy and slippery ground up to Carn Glas-choire – there is no path on this stretch. There are panoramic views of the Cairngorms from the top, which is a trig point.

Nearby

Visit the site of the 1746 Battle of Culloden, which was the last pitched battle fought on British soil. The battle took place on the moorland around Culloden, near Inverness and was the final battle in the Jacobite rising against Hanoverian rule. www.nts.org.uk/Culloden

▲ THE SUMMIT OF CARN GLAS-CHOIRE, LOOKING SOUTH

▲ LOOKING SOUTH TOWARDS THE CAIRNGORMS FROM CARN GLAS-CHOIRE

Norfolk

Beacon Hill_#85

105m | 344ft   26ᵗʰ | 07/09/08 | with Alex

Even the flattest of counties has a high point! In Norfolk's case, this is Beacon Hill near the north coast. A mixture of grass and woodland, it lies in an area of 'hilly' ground called the Cromer Ridge, a number of small hills formed by glacial moraine which lie along the coast near the town of Cromer. Beacon Hill is the tallest by some way, and unlike the majority of the county tops in the UK, offers views out to sea. The high point itself is unremarkable – it is one of just five in the country to lie on a road (the others being Huntingdonshire, Middlesex, Nottinghamshire and Suffolk). Alex and I visited on a wet day and it is fair to say we were underwhelmed by the site ...

But Norfolk is a lovely county, with a distinctive character. Its county town, Norwich, was until the Industrial Revolution Britain's second largest city, gaining its wealth from the wool industry. Today, it is (relatively speaking) much smaller, but retains its importance to the region, with some lovely old buildings (the cathedral and the castle), medieval streets and one of the largest markets in Europe.

It is, however, Norfolk's countryside and coastline which make Norfolk special. The stretch of coast between Hunstanton and Cley is particularly beautiful: the skies are big, the air fresh and there is excellent local beer in the many good gastropubs. Further south are the Norfolk Broads – a network of rivers and lakes, interspersed with wetlands and dotted with several windmills, some of which serve as windpumps, used to drain areas of land. The Broads are not actually a natural feature, but were created by medieval peat excavations in the Middle Ages. Today, they are a protected area and a popular tourist destination.

Start/parking: Radio mast near West Runton

Satnav: NR27 9NW (not exact)	**Start GR:** TG 186413	**High Point GR:** TG 186413
OS Map: Landranger 133 North East Norfolk		
Distance: N/A	**Ascent:** N/A	**Time:** N/A

Cafe/Pub: There are many cafes in nearby Cromer and Sheringham. You can get lovely crab sandwiches at the Joyful West's shellfish bar in Sheringham High Street (01263 825444). Further afield, The Walpole Arms at Itteringham is an excellent gastropub (01263 587258).

Directions

Park by the radio mast next to the minor road 1km S of West Runton, and 3km WSW of Cromer. This is Norfolk's high point and is unmarked.

Nearby

Visit the pleasant village of Holt (ten kilometres west-south-west) and the impressive house and gardens of Blickling Hall (fifteen kilometres south).

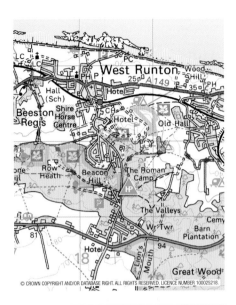

▲ THE BEACH AT CROMER IN NORFOLK

BY: LINDA STEWARD

Arbury Hill_#76

225m | 738ft   27th | 11/09/08 | with Harry

Northamptonshire lies just east of Birmingham and takes its name from the county town of Northampton. Referenced in the eighth century as 'Ham Tune', it had become 'Northantone' by the time of the Domesday book and 'Northamptone' by the thirteenth century – the prefix 'north' being added to separate it from the other 'Hamptons'.

Northamptonshire is known as 'Rose of the Shires' but also as a county of spires and squires. The renowned architectural historian Sir Nikolaus Pevsner famously put the churches and notable buildings of Northamptonshire on the map in one of his *The Buildings of England* series of county-by-county guides, highlighting their special qualities which hitherto had been little recognised.

The county top is Arbury Hill, a grassy hill rising gently out of the surrounding fields. The top features a square earthworks, some 200 metres across, in the form of a ditch and an embankment, which it is thought are all that remains of an Iron Age fort.

Despite being only 225 metres high, Arbury Hill forms a drainage divide between the catchment areas for three rivers – the Nene, Cherwell and Leam, the latter two running into the Severn and Thames respectively. It was perhaps fitting, then, that the walk to the top was across very lush fields and Harry and I rolled up our trouser legs to avoid getting wet!

Start/parking: Road verge near Badby

Satnav: BADBY	**Start GR:** SP 547587	**High Point GR:** SP 540587
OS Map: Landranger 152 Northampton & Milton Keynes		
Distance: 2km	**Ascent:** 50m	**Time:** 1hr
Cafe/Pub: Several available in nearby Daventry.		

Directions

Start 500m W of the A361, on the verge of the minor road from Badby to Upper Catesby, some 5km SW of Daventry.

Follow the bridleway WSW by the side of fields for 500m, and then go N for 200m up to the top of Arbury Hill. The top is unmarked.

Nearby

Visit Sulgrave Manor, which has connections with the first American President George Washington. One of his ancestors (Lawrence Washington) was Mayor of Northampton at the time of Henry VIII, and bought Sulgrave Manor from him. Or maybe visit the Silverstone motor racing circuit for the British Grand Prix.

▲ FLAGSTONE PATH ACROSS THE PEAT BOG ON TOP OF THE CHEVIOT

The Cheviot_#23

815m | 2,674ft   81st | 27/05/11 | solo

Right in the north-east corner of England, Northumberland borders Scotland. Unsurprisingly, therefore, it has been the scene of more than a few battles over the years – and contains the pretty town of Berwick-upon-Tweed, the former county town of the Scottish Berwickshire (p64). Reflecting this rather violent history, Northumberland boasts more castles than any other county in England.

To wander through Northumberland today, you'd not think of the past battles. It is a county with wonderful countryside, low-lying near the coast and rising dramatically as you move north-west, inland, towards the high point, The Cheviot.

Most people have heard of The Cheviot. It lies right at the top of the county, in the Cheviot Hills – a huge range of grass-and-scrub-covered hills with a wonderfully empty feel about them. (Northumberland is the most sparsely populated county in Britain.) The northern end of the Pennine Way runs across the Cheviots, right along the England/ Scotland border and up to The Cheviot, before dropping down to end nine kilometres away in Kirk Yetholm.

The route up The Cheviot was less demanding than I had anticipated and I was surprised to find how boggy it was on top – so much so that stone paving slabs were laid for about a mile. The peat covering the top of the mountain seemed like a cap placed on top. The summit is a trig point, which, unusually, is on top of a big five-foot high plinth. This substantial underpinning was apparently put in place after two previous trig points had sunk into the peat bog!

Apparently there are the remains of several aeroplanes near to The Cheviot – these crashes were due to navigation difficulties in bad weather many years ago. I combined this trip with a walk to Roxburghshire's high point (Hangingstone Hill, p206), which is just a mile away.

Start/parking: Grassy layby at NT 954225

Satnav: WOOLER (nearest)	**Start GR:** NT 953224	**High Point GR:** NT 909205

OS Map: Landranger 74 Kelso & Coldstream; Landranger 75 Berwick-upon-Tweed

Distance: 11km	**Ascent:** 600m	**Time:** 6hrs

Cafe/Pub: Breeze cafe in Wooler high street and the Copper Kettle Tea Rooms in Bamburgh are good spots for tea. Further afield, Battlesteads in Wark and Barn Asia in Newcastle are good dinner options.

▲ THE CHEVIOT HILLS

Directions

Start approx. 7km SW of Wooler and 800m NE of Langleeford on grassland (which is used as a car park) next to the minor road alongside Harthope Burn.

Walk 400m SW towards Langleeford to the edge of a wood. At a signpost towards Scald Hill, cross a stile and take the footpath briefly NW then W. This leads steadily upwards over grassland and moorland for 2.5km to Scald Hill. Continue along the path for 1.5km SW along the S side of the fence up the E side of The Cheviot; this path gets steeper the higher you go. On reaching the summit plateau the ground becomes so boggy that paving stones have been laid, and it is an easy stroll WSW along these for 500m to The Cheviot summit. The top is a trig point on top of a plinth.

To return, continue SW along the paving stones for 1km as far as Cairn Hill. Then cross the fence on the S side and head SSE downwards on the path along the E side of a fence for 500m to the head of Harthope Burn. Pick up the footpath at the head and follow this NE – this leads for 6km down the valley past Harthope Linn waterfall, Langleeford Hope and Langleeford back to the start. The first half of this stretch is along a rather messy footpath and the second half a bridleway; the messiness of the first half means it is easier, and a better option, to go down the route than up it.

From Cairn Hill there is a good detour W along paving stones and boardwalks to Hanging-stone Hill (Roxburghshire's high point, p206) and Auchope Cairn, which has superb views over Roxburghshire.

Nearby

Visit Hadrian's Wall and Vindolanda, where the famous Roman Vindolanda Writing Tablets (now in the British Museum) were found. Or Alnwick Castle (of Harry Potter fame). A little further afield is the somewhat special Holy Island, Lindisfarne, which can be visited at low tide. www.lindisfarne.org.uk

▲ LOOKING OVER THE CHEVIOT HILLS FROM CAIRN HILL

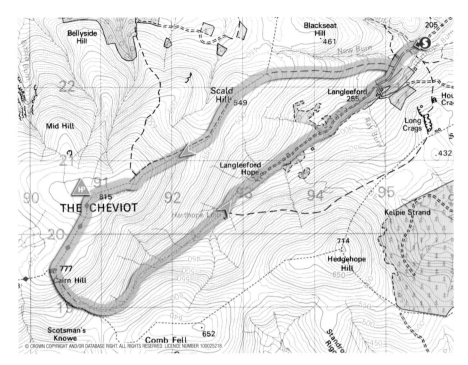

▲ THE CHEVIOT'S REINFORCED SUMMIT, PREVIOUS TRIG POINTS HAVING SUNK INTO THE PEAT BOG!

Nottinghamshire

Newtonwood Lane_#78

205m | 673ft   14ᵗʰ | 22/07/08 | with Alex

The area now known as Nottinghamshire was first settled in the fifth century, first named as a shire in the eleventh century and first mapped in 1576. Sitting fairly centrally in England it has, like the counties around it, a strong history of mining – which has, as we shall see, affected its high point.

A wonderful fifteenth-century poem opens with the line: *'Robyn hode in scherewode stod'.* Think of Nottingham and you think of Sherwood Forest and Robin Hood, the heroic nobleman who, deprived of his lands, turned outlaw, robbing the rich and giving to the poor. Whether or not Robin Hood actually existed is unknown. Details of the 'legend' have changed dramatically over the years, the only record of a 'Robin Hood' is from a village in Derbyshire and the Major Oak in Sherwood, the huge tree in which Hood was said to have hidden, would have been a mere sapling at the time. Some suggest that Robin Hood was an entirely fictional character; others that the name was one given to any outlaw.

The county top of Nottinghamshire is, like Robin Hood, disputed. Initially, it was claimed to be Silverhill Wood, which was recognised as such by the county council, who placed a plaque and statue of a coal miner on the spot. However, others believe that Newtonwood Lane, two feet higher and one kilometre away, takes the crown. Even then, it should be noted that both of these points are man-made – spoil heaps left over from Nottinghamshire's mining past. The highest natural point is Strawberry Bank in the nearby village of Huthwaite, which measures 203 metres. As the highest physical point, I visited Newtonwood Lane, and found it memorable for being a road above the Tibshelf service station on the M1 motorway. One of the great little pleasures of my *High Point* project has been to discover places such as this!

Start/parking: Newtonwood Lane

Satnav: DE55 5SG (nearest)	**Start GR:** SK 456604	**High Point GR:** SK 456606
OS Map: Landranger 120 Mansfield & Worksop		
Distance: N/A	**Ascent:** N/A	**Time:** N/A
Cafe/Pub: Try the Hardwick Inn at Hardwick Hall (01246 850245, www.hardwickinn.co.uk).		

Directions

Park at the top (NE end) of Newtonwood Lane by the reservoir compound. This is approx. 1km E of the Tibshelf service station on the M1, and is Nottinghamshire's high point. There are unremarkable views over the Tibshelf service station and its surrounding area. This is one of just five county high points accessible by road (the others are Norfolk, Suffolk, Middlesex and Huntingdonshire).

Nearby

Visit the superb Elizabethan Hardwick Hall, where Bess of Hardwick lived, the richest woman in England at the time after Elizabeth I. Further afield, visit the ancient pines at Edwinstowe in Sherwood Forest, and the nearby Major Oak, a huge, 800-year-old tree said to have been the hiding place of Robin Hood.

▲ THE 800-YEAR-OLD MAJOR OAK IN SHERWOOD FOREST

BY: CHRIS CAFFERKEY

Orkney Islands

Ward Hill_#57

481m | 1,578ft   72nd | 12/09/10 | solo

Lying some ten kilometres off the coast of Scotland, just north of John o'Groats, the Orkney Islands are a long way north. Consisting of about 70 islands, the largest – known as 'Mainland' – is home to around 20,000 people, while the smallest, Inner Holm, has a population of just one. There is evidence that the Orkney Islands have been visited by humans since Neolithic times and one of the most northerly islands, Papa Westray, actually contains the oldest preserved house in Northern Europe, a small stone farmstead called the Knap of Howar.

As you'd expect, the sea has a strong influence on the islands. The weather, for example, is surprisingly mild and stable, usually varying by only about ten degrees over the year – although strong winds are common. These winds are one reason for a striking lack of trees on the Orkney Islands, which are notably bare. Tens of thousands of seabirds nest on the islands' cliffs, and fishing is common; Orkney has the largest crab processing plant in the UK.

The Orkneys (and the Shetland Isles too) are a far more special place than I had imagined before my visit – so much so that they have both become around the top of my list of favourite counties. Alex and I were on Orkney for four days and visited some superb and surprising places – top of the list were the Old Man of Hoy; the Neolithic UNESCO World Heritage sites of Skara Brae, Maeshowe and the Ring of Brodgar; the dramatic Yesnaby cliffs; the remarkable Italian Chapel (decorated by Italian prisoners of war); the Broch of Durness; and Stromness.

It was a happy accident that the Orkneys' high point – Ward Hill – is on Hoy as it meant I could easily visit the Old Man of Hoy, which has been a minor ambition of mine ever since I saw live footage of Chris Bonington's ascent in the 1960s. Unlike Chris, I restricted my climbing to the high point, finding the view (across Scapa Flow) from the top to be among the best on all my trips.

I was somewhat anxious in the run-up to my visit to Ward Hill, as I had read several reports of people being aggressively dive-bombed by Bonxies (Great Skuas), who are very protective of their offspring. In the end I took evasive action, leaving my visit to September and avoiding the breeding season. This proved quite successful (although I was 'buzzed' a couple of times on my walk – quite an alarming experience) and I enjoyed a quiet walk on which I met no one other than a couple of inquisitive Bonxies and a mountain hare.

Start/parking: Minor road near Sandy Loch

Satnav: KW16 3NJ (nearest)	**Start GR:** HY 222033	**High Point GR:** HY 228022

OS Map: Landranger 6 Orkney – Mainland; Landranger 7 Orkney – Southern Isles

Distance: 5.5km	**Ascent:** 380m	**Time:** 3.5hrs

Cafe/Pub: You can get a cup of tea in the excellent Lyness World War II museum.

Directions

Start from the verge of the minor road where it turns N 90 degrees, just NE of Sandy Loch on Hoy. The car ferry from the Orkney mainland goes from Houton to Lyness, which is at the SE tip of Hoy. In the busy summer months a place will need to be reserved to guarantee a journey on the ferry.

Follow the trail SW for 2km past the N shore of Sandy Loch. Stop when the trail starts descending shortly after crossing the Burn of Redglen. Climb steeply SE for 1km until you reach the 358m spot point. Continue E for 500m to the 420m spot point and then NNE for 1.5km to the summit of Ward Hill. The top is a cairn from which there are stunning views over Scapa Flow.

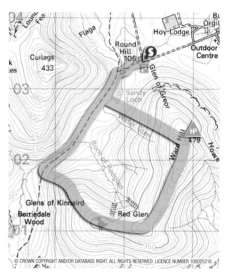

To return, you can go down the steep grassy hill to the NW. Go NW for 1km to the S end of Sandy Loch as far as the footpath, then retrace it NE for 600m back to the start point. Beware the possibility in the summer months of being dive-bombed by Bonxies (Great Skuas), protective of their offspring.

Nearby

On Hoy there are two gems – the Old Man of Hoy, which is a quite easy walk from Rackwick (6km return); and the World War II museum at Lyness.

▲ ST JOHN'S HEAD SEEN FROM BESIDE THE OLD MAN OF HOY

▲ GRAEMSAY AND SCAPA FLOW FROM WARD HILL

Oxfordshire

Whitehorse Hill_#72

261m | 856ft   10th | 20/06/08 | solo

An ancient county, Oxfordshire in southern England has long been associated with learning – most obviously through my alma mater, Oxford University. Records suggest that people have been teaching on the site of the university since 1096, although it is less clear as to the actual date of its foundation. It is, however, the oldest English-speaking university in the world and is consistently ranked in the top half dozen universities worldwide.

The county also pushes the boundaries of technology. Four of the eleven teams competing in the 2013 Formula 1 championship are based in the county, with another four located nearby. Why are they here? During WWII, a large number of aerospace engineers were based in the area. Once the war was over, they needed work, and found it in the motor industry, with their now-defunct airfields being perfect for testing cars. Now the area is a booming centre of engineering expertise.

Away from the books and workshops, Oxfordshire is a beautiful county. The county town of Oxford – the 'city of dreaming spires' – is full of beautiful architecture and lovely buildings. The River Thames flows through the south of the county, passing through Henley, home to the Henley Regatta and a very pretty village. To the west, the Cotswolds lie partially within the county, their rolling green hills and picturesque villages offering classically 'English' views.

The county top of Whitehorse Hill takes its name from the Uffington white horse, which lies on its north side. The horse is one of the most iconic chalk figures on the British Isles, a highly-stylised, 110-metre-long figure that requires an impressive 3,000 man hours each year to keep clean. Dating from the Bronze Age, it is by far the oldest white horse in the UK. The horse is only one of a number of ancient remains in the area. The strangely-named Wayland's Smithy is nearby, a Neolithic long barrow and chamber tomb. It sits just off the Ridgeway, a long distance national trail that follows a chalk ridge used by pre-historic man and is sometimes described as Britain's oldest road.

Start/parking: Woolstone Hill car park

Satnav: SN7 7QL (nearest)	**Start GR:** SU 293866	**High Point GR:** SU 300863

OS Map: Landranger 174 Newbury & Wantage

Distance: 1.5km	**Ascent:** 30m	**Time:** 1hr

Cafe/Pub: The appropriately-named Whitehorse in Woolstone is within walking distance (01367 820726, www.whitehorsewoolstone.co.uk). There is also a good gastropub at the Mole Inn in Toot Baldon (01865 340001, www.moleinn.com).

Directions

Start from the car park on Woolstone Hill, 1km S of Woolstone and just off the B4507, 10km W of Wantage.

Follow the track ESE for 500m up to the Uffington Castle fort. The summit of Whitehorse Hill is just to the E of the fort. The top is a trig point. There are panoramic views over the Vale of the Whitehorse.

Nearby

As mentioned opposite, there are a number of ancient sites in the region – a Neolithic fort and burial mounds on the hill itself and Wayland's Smithy and the Ridgeway trail nearby. Follow the Ridgeway south (a long way south!) and you reach Avebury, site of one of the most impressive stone circles in the country. Further afield, visit Oxford (particularly its lovely golden Cotswold stone colleges and other buildings, its Christchurch Meadow and its covered market), Cogges Manor Farm near Witney, where my son Harry spoke his first words some twenty years ago (pig in 'ere!), or the pretty village of Burford.

▲ THE TOP OF WHITEHORSE HILL

▲ LOOKING NORTH OVER OXFORDSHIRE FROM WHITEHORSE HILL

Broad Law_ #18

840m | 2,756ft   Joint 40th | 30/04/09 | solo

In 1975 Peebles-shire was merged with Berwickshire, Roxbughshire, Selkirkshire and Midlothian to form the Scottish Borders. It now forms the northern end of the modern-day county, sitting roughly halfway between Edinburgh and the border with England.

The county top, Broad Law, lies in the south of the county, on the boundary with Selkirkshire. It is not only the county top of both counties, but also the highest point in their successor, the Scottish Borders council area, and the second highest peak in the Southern Uplands of Scotland. Beautifully open and clear in summer, it is spectacularly bleak in winter, and surprisingly remote and wild-feeling. Despite being relatively accessible and close to some major roads, there is little traffic in the immediate area and I met no one on my way to the top.

The route to the top begins at the Megget Stone, a megalithic standing stone which is thought to have been used as a boundary marker, lying, like the county top, on the county boundary. Despite its name, history and marker status, it is considerably less impressive than the peak above, standing a mere three feet high, in a grassy field.

Having left the Stone, the route to the top is straightforward, following a fence-line all the way up. While much of the Border country is covered in heather moor, the terrain here is shortish grass, making for a relatively easy ascent – although, this does, of course, depend on the route taken: while Broad Law, in common with many of the surrounding peaks, is a smooth and rounded hill, some of the neighbouring valleys have particularly steep sides.

Start/parking: Megget Stone
Satnav: ML12 6QS (nearest)   **Start GR:** NT 150203   **High Point GR:** NT 146235
OS Map: Landranger 72 Upper Clyde Valley
Distance: 6.5km   **Ascent:** 390m   **Time:** 3.5hrs
Cafe/Pub: Approximately 12 kilometres east, at the northern tip of the Loch of the Lowes, is the Glen Cafe – a beautiful spot for a post-walk cup of tea. Nearby, in Hawick High Street, is the excellent Turnbull's coffee house.

Directions

Start from the Megget Stone (you can park on the south verge next to a cattle grid) on the minor road from Tweedsmuir to Cappercleuch. This road connects the A701 with the A708.

Follow the fence NW for 500m up to Fans Law (this fence goes all the way to the Broad Law summit).

Continue N for 3km up to Cairn Law and then Broad Law. The top is a trig point next to the fence. You will be able to see (weather permitting) a radio beacon station nearby to the north.

Nearby

About twenty kilometres west is the Dumfries-shire high point, White Coomb, and the dramatic Grey Mare's Tail waterfall at its base. Why not combine the two (as I did)? Alternatively, head back past Tweeds-muir (stopping to admire the view over Talla Reservoir) and drive south a short way on the A701 to Tweed's Well, the source of the River Tweed. Apparently one of the 'great salmon fishing rivers' of Scotland, it drains the entire Border region on its way to the east coast near Berwick-upon-Tweed. Also visit the interesting towns of Peebles, Hawick (noted for its cashmere industry) and Moffat.

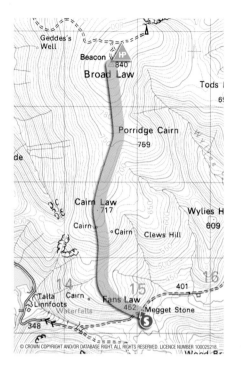

▲ THE SUMMIT OF BROAD LAW

▲ ON BROAD LAW

Pembrokeshire

Foel Cwmcerwyn_#49

536m | 1,759ft

South Wales's Pembroke coast is hugely popular with tourists. The majority come for the sandy beaches, quiet bays and seaside towns, while some travel for the sea-cliff rock climbing, the walking (the Coast Path National Trail runs for almost 300 kilometres along the cliff tops) and the Pembrokeshire Coast National Park – the only coastal park of its kind. Other visitors are drawn by the towns: St David's, the smallest city in Britain; Tenby, the walled seaside town on the south coast; and Pembroke, the former county town with its medieval castle.

County-toppers should head for the Preseli Hills in the north of the county. A ten-kilometre ridge of blunt, round hilltops and small rocky outcrops, they feel worlds away from the bustling coast. The hills are dotted with prehistoric remnants: Neolithic burial chambers, standing stones and Iron Age forts. Amazingly, they are also a possible source for the bluestones that make up the inner circle of Stonehenge, 180 miles away.

The county top, Foel Cwmcerwyn, is just off the main ridge of hills, marked by a trig point. The summit is open, rounded and grassy, with a few tufts of reed-like grass. The ground underfoot was very wet on my visit, at least in part due to heavy rains the day before (when I visited Fan Foel, Carmarthenshire's high point, p84). The route to the top begins on heathland, then skirts the edge of Pantmaenog Forest before breaking out onto the open grassland of the top.

Start/parking: Car park on B4329

Satnav: SA66 7RA (nearest)	**Start GR:** SN 075322	**High Point GR:** SN 094311

OS Map: Landranger 145 Cardigan & Mynydd Preseli

Distance: 6km	**Ascent:** 130m	**Time:** 2.5hrs

Cafe/Pub: The odd-looking Tafarn Sinc, virtually beneath the high point in the village of Rosebush (01437 532214, www.tafarnsinc.co.uk).

Directions

Start from the car park on the B4329, 3km NE of the crossroads at New Inn. The car park is on the Mynydd Preseli ridge.

Follow the track E along the north end of Pantmaenog Forest. The track becomes indistinct and boggy after a while. After 2km, just past the end of the woods, the track splits. Follow the track S for 1km to Foel Cwmcerwyn. The top is a trig point.

Nearby

You're in the Pembrokeshire Coast National Park – the only coastal national park in Britain. Try the 186-mile coastal path, which runs the length of the county's coastline or, for something shorter (!), walk the splendid bridleway along the top of the Preseli Hills from Cerrig Lladron to Foel Drygarn.

▲ THE SUMMIT OF FOEL CWMCERWYN

▲ LOOKING ACROSS PEMBROKESHIRE FROM FOEL CWMCERWYN

Ben Lawers_#4

1,214m | 3,983ft   43rd | 13/05/09 | solo

Once known as the 'big county', Perthshire sits in the middle of Scotland, on the southern edge of the Highlands. It was named not only for its sheer size, but also for the diversity of its towns and countryside. Full of hills and lochs, castles and distilleries, it is a fascinating county to visit. In the south lies Perth, the county town and former capital of Scotland, thanks in part to Scone Palace, home to the Stone of Scone ('Stone of Destiny'), where Scottish kings were crowned up to 1296, before King Edward I of England moved the Stone to London. The stone has now been returned to Scotland, and resides in Edinburgh Castle, alongside the Scottish crown jewels.

Away from Perth, inland, are the mountains. To the north are the Cairngorms, and to the west and north-west are the Grampians. The Grampians run across highland Scotland from north–east to south–west, and it is here that Perthshire's county top, Ben Lawers, is found. At nearly 4,000 feet, Ben Lawers is the third highest county top, and the tenth highest peak in Britain. As such, it felt like an important mountain to tackle in my high point pursuit.

The mountain lies on a long ridge which includes seven Munros (to walk the ridge would be a fantastic, but long, day out!). Only 17 feet short of the 4,000-feet mark, there was an attempt made in the late nineteenth century to build a large cairn atop the summit and thus reach the magic height. As the cairn is long gone and the Ordnance Survey ignored it anyway, the work was all for nothing.

I climbed Ben Lawers on a clear day and could see countless mountains in the distance. About halfway up I had the embarrassment of being overtaken by a 70-year-old man. I felt better when he told me he had previously completed all 284 Munros and was now halfway round a second circuit – he must have been very fit for his age!

Start/parking: Ben Lawers Nature Reserve car park

Satnav: FK21 8TY (nearest)   **Start GR:** NN 608379   **High Point GR:** NN 635414

OS Map: Landranger 51 Loch Tay & Glen Dochart

Distance: 8km   **Ascent:** 780m   **Time:** 6hrs

Cafe/Pub: The Old Smiddy cafe/bistro in Killin serves good teas and dinners (01567 820619, www.theoldsmiddykillin.co.uk).

Directions

Start from the Ben Lawers National Nature Reserve car park. This is 2km (just over halfway) up the minor road from the A827 to the Lochan na Lairige reservoir.

Follow the track NNE up the Burn of Edramucky. For the first 1.5km this is within a fenced off area (fenced off to protect it from deer). After exiting this area, continue on the track NE for 1.5km steeply upwards to the top of Beinn Ghlas (1,103m). Then follow the ridge (this can be very windy at times) NE for a further 1.5km up to the top of Ben Lawers. The top is a trig point. There are panoramic views in all directions from the top.

Return by retracing your steps for 0.5km and then bear right on a lovely path over grassy slopes, skirting the north of Beinn Ghlas and then following the Burn of Edramucky SSW back down to the fenced off area.

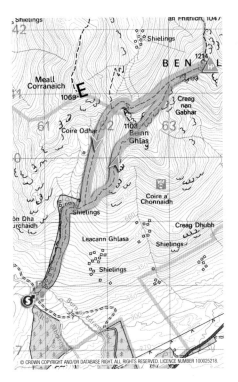

Nearby

Visit Scone Palace (see opposite) on the outskirts of Perth (www.scone-palace.co.uk). Or visit Blair Castle at Blair Atholl, which dates back to 1269 and is rich in Scottish history (www.blair-castle.co.uk).

▲ THE TOP OF SCOTLAND FROM BEN LAWERS

▲ LOOKING EAST FROM BEN LAWERS TOWARDS LOCH TAY

Great Rhos_#39

660m | 2,165ft   74ᵗʰ | 17/09/10 | solo

Central Wales is a wonderfully bleak and wild place. From the hilltops, it is virtually impossible to see any sign of human habitation. No towns, no houses, no roads ... In fact, not only are there few people, but the largest town in the area, Llandrindod Wells, has a tiny population of under 6,000. The entire county has just 25,000 residents. But that is the great appeal of this area – the quietness, the hills and the wildlife.

The county top, Great Rhos, sits in Radnor Forest – a forest that isn't actually a forest. True, there is managed woodland in the area, but the term actually refers to a large dome of land, topped by Great Rhos. It is only a 'forest' in the sense of being a medieval hunting area. (Royal Hunting Forests were areas of land which supported significant numbers of game animals and were thus ideal for hunting. In the eleventh century, Norman Kings placed several of these areas under 'Forest Law' in order to protect the stock of game, creating the Hunting Forests and arousing a degree of resentment from those who lived and worked in the affected regions.)

Great Rhos itself is a broad, grassy peak with a boggy, heathery summit plateau. There is no path, nor any distinguishing feature, near the top, which I imagine would be tricky to find in mist. The east side of the hill drops away dramatically into a steep-sided valley, while the western and northern edges descend more gradually, offering expansive views over the surrounding area.

According to legend, the last dragon in Wales is said to lie sleeping beneath the hills of Radnor Forest, kept there by a ring of churches built by local people. If the churches are destroyed, it is said, the dragon will wake – tread carefully!

Start/parking: The centre of New Radnor

Satnav: LD8 2SN	**Start GR:** SO 212608	**High Point GR:** SO 182639
OS Map: Landranger 148 Presteigne & Hay-on-Wye		
Distance: 9km	**Ascent:** 430m	**Time:** 4.5hrs

Cafe/Pub: Emily's Tearooms in nearby Presteigne is a nice cafe. For a first class dinner, the Stagg Inn at Titley is well worth a visit.

Directions

Start in New Radnor. Follow the B4372 SW to the A44, and then along to Haine's Mill, 1km from New Radnor.

Take the track NW along the side of the mill and by a stream for 700m to Lower Harley. Then cross the stream and take the path NW up the hillside. Beyond the woods at Upper Harley you will encounter danger signs, which relate to munitions testing, regularly all the way to the top – however, the path follows the western boundary of the danger area so the route is safe. After 1km the path passes through a disused quarry. Continue NW then N for 2km until the path reaches a fence. Cross the fence then head 300m NW across heathery boggy ground to the summit. There is no clear path on this part of the route; the area is featureless and it could be tricky to find the summit in mist. The top is a trig point.

Nearby

Visit the county town, Presteigne – a nice little town, with the self-styled title of the 'Gateway to Wales' (there are many other such gateways too). It is a beautiful small town to visit, with an award-winning museum and two annual music and arts festivals.

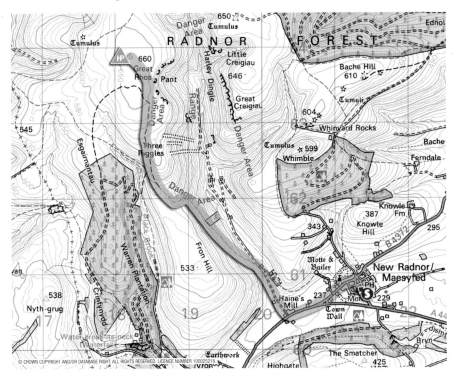

▲ THE HARLEY DINGLE DANGER AREA FROM ABOVE UPPER HARLEY

198   HIGH POINT

Hill of Stake_#53

522m | 1,713ft   88ᵗʰ | 20/07/12 | with Lesley Bryce

Renfrewshire took a break from county status in 1975, becoming part of Strathclyde. Strathclyde, however, only lasted twenty years and was abolished in 1996, at which point Renfrewshire returned – albeit at less than half its original size. Lying just west of Glasgow it is, in terms of area, one of the smallest counties in the UK, but is one of the busiest in population. However, this is Scotland, and so there are still several lovely areas of remote countryside.

The strangely-named county top, the Hill of Stake, is in one such area within the Clyde Muirshiel Regional Park, a large area of land on the coast. The county top is right in the centre of the park and, despite lying around twenty miles west of Glasgow, it is a remote spot. Covered by heathery, boggy moorland, there is no path within a mile of the summit – only tussocky, lumpy ground.

It took me three visits to climb the hill successfully. My first visit was a washout – I had to abandon the trip without getting out of the car as the weather was so foul. My second visit was a disaster – I broke my leg when on the way up the hill, about 400 metres from the top, when stepping in one of the many hidden holes in the ground. I then had to negotiate the major emergency which ensued – in the mist, miles from anywhere and anyone, without a mobile phone signal. My third, and last, visit was eleven months later, when it was a case of 'third time lucky'. This time I went in good weather and was accompanied by the excellent Lesley Bryce, who is a professional mountain guide based in nearby Ayrshire.

The successful third visit turned out to be something of a release for me – the eleven months after my leg break had been a great trial, first recovering from the break (which took over six months) and then dealing with a feeling of angst in my mind thereafter; not a day went by in that entire eleven month period when I did not at some point worry about my accident and its consequences. So I was naturally very glad to exorcise my demons by successfully completing the climb without incident on 20 July 2012. As so often, we met no-one on the walk.

Notwithstanding its modest height, the Hill of Stake is undoubtedly the 'bête noire' of all the mountains which I walked on my *High Point* project.

Start/parking: Muirshiel Country Park visitor centre

Satnav: PA12 4LB (nearest)	**Start GR:** NS 311632	**High Point GR:** NS 273630

OS Map: Landranger 63 Firth of Clyde

Distance: 9km	**Ascent:** 260m	**Time:** 4.5hrs

Cafe/Pub: Although refreshments are available at the visitor centre, Nardini's in Largs is the place to go, and is Scotland's holy grail for Italian ice cream (01475 675000, www.nardinis.co.uk).

Directions

Start from the Muirshiel Country Park visitor centre, about 5km NW of Lochwinnoch.

Follow the track NW from the visitor centre for 200m until you reach the disused bridge over the River Calder. Cross the bridge and head W, then WNW, for 1.7km steadily upwards over boggy, grassy ground up to the top of Queenside Hill (472m). Then head WSW for 2km to the Hill of Stake; the route goes over heathery, boggy, uneven ground and a couple of burns (White Grain Burn and Wee Burn), then rises steeply (but straightforwardly) up the grassy slopes of the Hill of Stake. The top is a trig point, with lovely views over to Arran, Ben Lomond and Glasgow.

Return via the now disused barytes mine: head NNE for 1.5km, initially down grassy slopes, then over heathery, boggy, uneven ground, then down next to a burn to the mine. There is no path along this route, so a bearing will need to be taken to be sure of the direction. Pick up the path at the top of the mineshafts and follow this NNE for 500m down the E side of the fenced-off burn. Then head E along the old miners' track and follow this for 3km back to the visitor centre – this is a straightforward, easy walk.

Note: The 3.5km route from Queenside Hill to the Hill of Stake, and from there to the barytes mine, has no footpath and is best walked in good weather, as route finding is difficult in low cloud or misty conditions. Also, the terrain is heathery, quite boggy and uneven with many hidden foot-sized holes, one of which caused me to break my leg on my second visit. So the walker needs to concentrate on his/her feet!

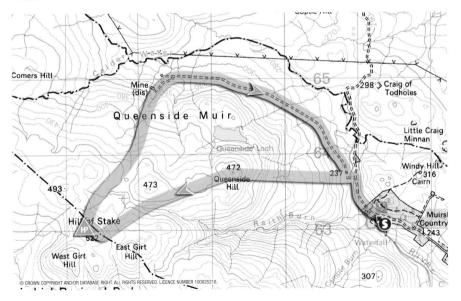

Càrn Eige_#5

1,183m | 3,881ft   44ᵗʰ | 03/06/09 | solo

With scenery as spectacular as you will see anywhere in Britain, Ross and Cromarty is an unforgettable county. One of the most remote areas in Scotland, there are few towns and virtually no roads, just beautiful lochs, mountains and wide open spaces. Its mountains consist of some of the oldest rock formations in Europe and are truly spectacular. The wildlife is equally special, with red deer, pine martens and otters all found in the area. If you're really lucky, you might spot a golden eagle or, closer to the coast, a seal or two.

The county stretches across the north of Scotland, starting near Loch Ness and passing through Glen Affric and Torridon as it runs west to the coast, where the historic county then crossed to the Isle of Lewis. The county no longer contains Lewis, but instead featuring the Isle of Skye, home to the Cuillin Ridge and the striking Old Man of Storr. With so few people, the economy of the county is mainly built around tourism, with fishing and crofting – where small areas of land are cultivated for small-scale food production – also featuring heavily and adding to the remote feel of the region.

Càrn Eige is in Glen Affric in a remote area north-west of Loch Ness. This area is a gem which is largely unknown to the countless tourists who speed down the side of the loch, and which I myself was barely aware of previously. It is visited by a dedicated minority of people as there are no through roads here. Glen Affric hosts a dozen or so Munros, so Munro-baggers will know it well. I found the area around Loch Affric amongst the most beautiful in all Scotland, with a big open feel to it. Càrn Eige is the fourth highest of the mountains on my list, so I was pleased to negotiate it successfully. In completing this route, I felt I had really experienced the best of the Highlands. Unforgettable.

Start/parking: Car park, Loch Affric

Satnav: IV4 7NB (nearest)   **Start GR:** NH 201233   **High Point GR:** NH 123261

OS Map: Landranger 25 Glen Carron & Glen Affric

Distance: 20km   **Ascent:** 1,210m   **Time:** 10.5hrs

Cafe/Pub: Pleasant tea and cakes at the Bog Cotton Cafe in Cannich Camping and Caravan Park.

Directions

Start from the car park at the eastern end of remote Loch Affric.

Follow the track W for 5.5km along and then above the northern shore of Loch Affric. Just before Allt Coire Leachavie take the track N then NW along the river and follow this for 3.5km to the col at the head of the valley. In the last section, before a steep rise to the col, the path crosses a moraine field. Head N then NE for 500m up to the big cairn at the top of the munro Mam Sodhail (1,181m). Continue N then NE to Càrn Eige, dropping 130m before rising a similar amount. The top is a trig point, with superb panoramic views.

Return to Mam Sodhail, then go ESE along the ridge to Mullach Cadha Rainich and then Sgurr na Lapaich. Head down SE then E for 2.5km (no path and boggy) as far as the hairpin bend in the path which is 1km NW of Affric Lodge. Follow the path E then S for 2km to Affric Lodge, and then E for 1.5km back to the start. A fantastic day out!

Nearby

From the high point walk's start point, you can walk on a path right around Loch Affric, a lovely walk; anti-clockwise is best. Further afield, heading west, visit Glen Torridon, with its stunning scenery, or drive round the Applecross peninsula, where you can park the car at 2,000 feet up and wander out from there. Stay at the Tigh an Eilean hotel in Shieldaig, aptly described by Alastair Sawday as the holy grail of Wester Ross hotels. Visit Inverewe Gardens, just north of Loch Maree. Head off to Skye – you can take the train from Inverness to Kyle of Lochalsh, and hire a car from there. Heading east, visit the Tain Pottery and Anta shop near Tain (both are signposted from the A9 south of Tain). Visit Cromarty, taking the tiny (four car) ferry from Nigg, and the Black Isle.

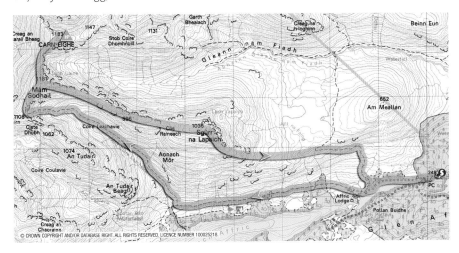

▲ LOCH AFFRIC AND MAM SODHAIL

BY: DEREK McDOUGALL

Roxburghshire

Hangingstone Hill_#32

743m | 2,438ft   82nd | 27/05/11 | solo

'Hangingstone Hill' is not actually marked on maps of Roxburghshire, but is there, none-the-less, sitting on the border between Scotland and England, in the Cheviot Hills. The Hills are an area of wild, empty land straddling the border, shared between Roxburghshire and Northumberland. Covered in rolling grassland and heather, they are a beautiful and remote place to visit.

Roxburghshire's high point is a spur of The Cheviot (Northumberland's top, p176) and is easily reached from that peak, walking along the flagstones and boardwalk of the Pennine Way, which are conveniently laid across the boggy ground. Of course, that does mean reaching a Scottish top from the English side! It takes its name from the 'hanging stone' – a small rocky outcrop which was used to mark the border between England and Scotland. It has a macabre history – apparently named after a man who, upon sitting on the rock, knocked his pack over the edge and strangled himself ...

I visited Hangingstone Hill having six months previously climbed Cauldcleuch Head (some fifty kilometres away) thinking, thanks to the Internet, that it was Roxburghshire's high point. It just goes to show you cannot believe everything you read! To add insult to injury, all was going well on that walk until near the end when I dropped down from Pennygant Hill and discovered I had to cross Billhope Burn. The burn was quite wide (three or four metres) and the only way to cross was to jump between damp and slimy rocks protruding from the water. Halfway across my foot slipped and I fell into the burn – not so bad, or indeed unusual, you might think, except that in this case my face ended up under water!

Start/parking: Grassy lay-by at NT 953224

Satnav: WOOLER (nearest)	**Start GR:** NT 953224	**High Point GR:** NT 895193

OS Map: Landranger 74 Kelso & Coldstream; Landranger 75 Berwick-upon-Tweed

Distance: 13km	**Ascent:** 640m	**Time:** 6.5hrs

Cafe/Pub: Breeze cafe in Wooler high street and the Copper Kettle Tea Rooms in Bamburgh are good spots for tea. Or alternatively, further afield, the excellent Turnbull's coffee house in Hawick High Street.

▲ LOOKING DOWN ON THE BILLHOPE BURN

Directions

Start approx. 7km SW of Wooler and 800m NE of Langleeford on grassland (which is used as a car park) next to the minor road alongside Harthope Burn.

Walk 400m SW towards Langleeford to the edge of a wood. At a signpost towards Scald Hill, cross a stile and take the footpath briefly NW then W. This leads steadily upwards over grassland and moorland for 2.5km to Scald Hill. Continue along the path for 1.5km SW along the S side of the fence up the E side of The Cheviot; this path gets steeper the higher you go. On reaching the summit plateau the ground becomes so boggy that paving stones have been laid, and it is an easy stroll WSW along these for 500m to The Cheviot summit. The top is a trig point on top of a plinth.

Continue over the summit and along the ridge to Cairn Hill. Follow paving stones, and then boardwalk W for 500m to Hangingstone Hill. The top is unmarked.

As a pleasant little detour, follow the boardwalk NW for 500m to Auchope Cairn, which has superb views over Roxburghshire.

To return, continue SW along the boardwalk and paving stones for 1km as far as Cairn Hill. Then cross the fence on the south side and head SSE downwards on the path along the E side of a fence for 500m to the head of Harthope Burn. Pick up the footpath at the head and follow this NE – this leads for 6km down the valley past Harthope Linn waterfall, Langleeford Hope and Langleeford back to the start. The first half of this stretch is along a rather messy footpath and the second half a bridleway; the messiness of the first half means it is easier, and a better option, to go down the route than up it.

Nearby

Visit the county town of Hawick (known for its cashmere industry), Jedburgh (dominated by the ruins of its abbey) or Kelso (which has a cobbled square and surrounding streets).

▲ AUCHOPE CAIRN

▲ THE TOP OF HANGINGSTONE HILL

© CROWN COPYRIGHT AND/OR DATABASE RIGHT. ALL RIGHTS RESERVED. LICENCE NUMBER 100025218.

Rutland

Cold Overton Park Wood_#79

197m | 646ft   13th | 21/07/08 | with Alex

England's smallest county sits centrally in the country, squeezed between Leicestershire, Northamptonshire and Lincolnshire. It has an excellent motto Multum in Parvo ('much in little'), which is spot-on – it's a rather interesting county with much to see and do. Compensating for its tiny size, Rutland is home to the country's largest man-made lake, Rutland Water (by surface area – but it is beaten capacity-wise by Kielder Water). The lake not only serves as a reservoir, but is widely used for recreation (it is popular with sailors and fishermen) and as a nature reserve – the most notable inhabitants being ospreys, which were re-introduced to the area in 1996, to great success.

The county was briefly abolished in 1974, becoming part of Leicestershire. This action was relatively short-lived, as Rutland was re-instated as a county 20 years later, in 1997. These changes did not affect too many people however, as the county only contains two towns – the county town of Oakham and the market town of Uppingham.

Oakham lies between Rutland Water and the county top, and is worth a visit if you're in the area, if only to visit Oakham Castle. One side of the castle's great hall is dominated by a display of large horseshoes. Look closely, and you'll notice something odd – they are all upside down. Bizarrely, all horseshoes in Rutland are apparently hung this way up, tips down. Elsewhere in the country, this is often considered to be bad luck; here, they are hung this way to prevent the devil from making a nest at the bottom of the shoe.

Another curiosity is the hamlet of Whitwell – one of the smallest villages in the county. Signs there suggest it is twinned with Paris, the capital of France. Apparently, this followed from a stunt in the 1970s when regulars from a local pub wrote to the then Mayor of Paris, Jacques Chirac, proposing the twinning link, but with a tight deadline for a response. As no answer was received by the set date, the village declared itself to be twinned!

Rutland's high point is labelled Cold Overton Park *Wood* but is, in fact, in open ground. Despite this, the trig point is not easy to find, sitting strangely halfway along the side of a flat field – it was thus a rather fun hunt for Alex and I to find.

Start/parking: Road verge		
Satnav: OAKHAM (nearest)	**Start GR:** SK 818092	**High Point GR:** SK 827085
OS Map: Landranger 141 Kettering & Corby		
Distance: 3km	**Ascent:** 40m	**Time:** 1hr
Cafe/Pub: There are several pubs and cafes in Oakham. Try the Lord Nelson, the Admiral Hornblower or the Grainstore.		

Directions

Start from the verge of the minor road which leads from Oakham to Knossington, at the junction with the road N to Cold Overton just past the 161m spot point.

Follow the road for 1km ESE to the radio relay station between Spring Farm and Glebe Farm. Turn S down the track which leads for 300m to a small reservoir and then 400m SSW across fields until reaching a fence heading NW. Follow this for 200m up to the top. The top is a trig point next to and on the S side of the fence.

Nearby

Rutland Water and Oakham are both nearby and worth visiting. You can cycle or walk around the lake, or visit the nature reserve (and if you're lucky, spot an osprey). In Oakham, visit the church or the castle (see opposite) – or I recommend the award-winning sausages and pork pies from the High Street's Leeson butchers, whose owner is most entertaining! Also visit Northfield Farm Shop and Cafe, which is about a third of the way from Oakham to Melton Mowbray; it was here that I nearly bought a yard of rye bread. There's also Uppingham and Stamford, known for its splendid stone buildings – both are pleasant towns to browse around.

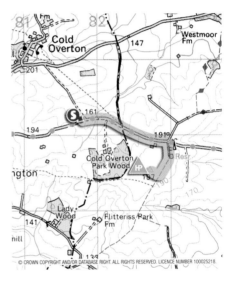

▲ COLD OVERTON PARK WOOD TRIG POINT

Selkirkshire

Broad Law_#18

840m | 2,756ft   Joint 40th | 30/04/09 | solo

Originally known as Ettrick Forest, Selkirkshire was once renowned for its heavy tree coverage. It was a Royal Forest – although this had nothing to do with woodland, being instead a designation given to areas that could support deer and game. These areas were effectively claimed by the monarch and hunting rights restricted so that only the royal family and aristocracy were allowed to hunt in the area. Over the years, Selkirkshire's tree coverage has reduced, partly to make way for sheep farming and partly due to industrial logging, and few traces remain. Despite this, Selkirkshire remains, along with the rest of the Borders region, a heavily rural region.

Broad Law, the county top of Selkirkshire, is also that of Peebles-shire (p188). Both counties are now merged, along with every other historic shire in the area, into the Scottish Borders – of which Broad Law is the high point. The term 'Scottish Borders' is a confusing one, referring here to the council area formed in 1975 by merging all the counties in the south-eastern corner of Scotland. The term is also used to mean the entire area along the southern edge of Scotland, with the historical 'Borders' also including the northernmost areas of England. Predictably, this is a region that has been subject to heavy fighting across the years, with Berwickshire and Roxburghshire bearing the brunt of the action as England and Scotland battled for land and power. To top it off, even when the two countries were not fighting one another, the region was harassed by the Border Reivers. These were groups of raiders, of both English and Scottish nationality, who, feeling little allegiance to either country, preyed indiscriminately on settlements across the entire Borders region. Today, the Reivers are remembered (and rather romanticised) through the writings of Sir Walter Scott, in folk songs and in annual festivals.

Start/parking: Megget Stone
Satnav: ML12 6QS (nearest)   **Start GR:** NT 150203   **High Point GR:** NT 146235
OS Map: Landranger 72 Upper Clyde Valley
Distance: 6.5km   **Ascent:** 390m   **Time:** 3.5hrs
Cafe/Pub: Approximately 12 kilometres east, at the northern tip of the Loch of the Lowes, is the Glen Cafe – a beautiful spot for a post-walk cup of tea.

Full details of the walk can be found on p188 for Peebles-shire.

Nearby

Head north to Selkirk, admiring the beautiful Borders scenery on the way. In 1298 the Scottish icon William Wallace was declared Guardian of Scotland in Selkirk, while, 500 years later, Sir Walter Scott sat as Sheriff of the town – his courtroom still stands. If you just want a bite to eat, the town is famous for its bannock, a type of dry fruitcake.

▲ ON BROAD LAW

Ronas Hill_#58

450m | 1,476ft   71ˢᵗ | 07/09/10 | solo

Fifty miles north of Orkney are the Shetland Islands, the most northerly point in the British Isles. They are far enough north, in fact, to be closer to the Arctic circle than London, for it never to become completely dark at midsummer and for the northern lights to be a regular sight.

The Shetlands are an archipelago of about 100 islands based around a substantial 'mainland' island, rising out of the water to rugged, heather-clad hills on the east and centre, and grassier regions to the west. The coasts are cut with deep, glacial sea inlets, or voes. The cliffs, some of the highest in Britain, are dotted with sea caves and interspersed by sandy beaches and are home to large colonies of seabirds, including puffins. You're almost guaranteed to see seals and porpoise in the surrounding seas, while the Shetlands are one of the best places to spot otters in the UK.

So far removed from the mainland, the Shetlands have, as you might expect, a unique and individual culture. Much of this is drawn from the islands' many years of Viking rule. Almost all the place names here are of Scandinavian origin and the musical-sounding language, with its impenetrable dialect, has definite Norse roots. Then there's the spectacular annual fire festival *Up Helly Aa*, held in Lerwick in midwinter, where, for twenty-four hours, the islanders dress as Vikings, burn a replica longship and dance the night away. The strong musical tradition found locally should feel a little more familiar however, with fiddle-playing featuring strongly.

The high point, Ronas Hill, is 450 metres above sea level on the Northmavine part of the Shetland mainland. The route to it is across a heavily-worn moonscape, smoothed by the high winds which are the norm on the islands. The summit is flat and rocky, topped by a hollowed-out cairn that is thought to have Neolithic origins.

The Shetland Islands were a treat to visit, far exceeding my expectations. The birdlife and natural scenery were fantastic and part of what make the islands so special. Unusual birds seem to be everywhere and the landscape is continually interesting. It seemed amusing that all the roads were spotless and perfectly maintained, as if built yesterday, presumably as a result of money from the nearby oil fields. Lonely Planet list the Shetlands in their 'top 10 must visit' destinations in the world – you might think that is a bit of a surprising assessment but, having visited, I can see why. Our visit was a constant delight.

Start/parking: Collafirth Hill radio masts

Satnav: N/A	**Start GR:** HU 335835	**High Point GR:** HU 305834

OS Map: Landranger 3 Shetland – North Mainland

Distance: 6km	**Ascent:** 170m	**Time:** 3hrs

Cafe/Pub: Good fish and chips at Frankie's in nearby Brae; it claims to be Britain's most northerly fish and chip shop (01806 522700). Also, a very tasty, Belgian-style dinner at Burrastow House, Walls (01595 809307).

Directions

Start from the radio masts at the top of Collafirth Hill. This is 2km from the A970 just north of North Collafirth.

Head ENE for 2km across rocky terrain to Roga Field and then to Mid Field. Then head SW for 1km past Shurgie Scord, across the Grud Burn and up Ronas Hill. The top is a trig point, near to a chambered cairn. There is no footpath on this walk, so if you cannot see the Ronas Hill summit, you will need to use a compass very carefully as the area is featureless. The terrain throughout is easy to negotiate but somewhat other-worldly – the ground is largely red granite gravel topped with sparse barren vegetation of very low growing heather and sub-alpine heath. Granite boulders are everywhere.

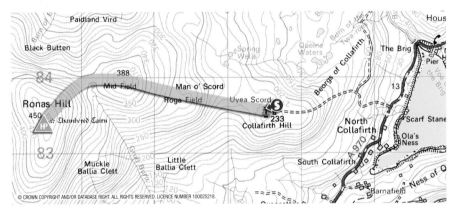

▲ LOOKING WEST FROM RONAS HILL

Brown Clee Hill_#48

540m | 1,772ft   73rd | 16/09/10 | with Alex

The name 'Shropshire' comes from the rather fantastic Old English 'Scrobbesbyrigscir' – which meant 'Shrewsburyshire'. And that isn't all that's interesting about Shropshire. Back in the thirteenth century, when the English parliament met for the first time, it was not at Westminster, but in Acton Burnell, a small village south of Shrewsbury. Also near Shrewsbury is Ditherington flax mill, the oldest iron-framed building in the world and the 'grandfather of skyscrapers', built in 1797. This was about the same time that England's coldest temperature was recorded – a chilly -25.2 degrees Celsius in Shawbury. It can't have been that cold on a regular basis the century before though, as that's when the sweet pea was first introduced to our plates, in the town of Wem.

There are two definite sides to Shropshire. The northern and central part of the county is relatively flat, with a great deal of fertile land and most of the county's towns. It has a strong industrial heritage, with several large coal mines and the Ironbridge gorge – an area rich in iron ore, coal and clay. It became an important centre of the industrial revolution, manufacturing porcelain and iron, and is now a UNESCO World Heritage Site. Ironbridge gorge and town are named after The Iron Bridge – the first cast iron bridge in the world and a scheduled ancient monument.

Meanwhile, a quarter of Shropshire is designated the Shropshire Hills Area of Natural Beauty, which lie in the south of the county. It is a lovely, rural area, with few towns and several significant ranges of hills – the Long Mynd, the Wrekin and the Clee Hills. It's the Clee Hills that we're interested in, as they contain the county high point, Brown Clee Hill. Lying about thirty miles west of Birmingham and on the Shropshire Way, Brown Clee Hill is on heathland which sits above Shropshire's lovely patchwork of fields. Covered in a mix of open grass and woodland, the view from the top is expansive, to say the least. Look east and you can see across England, almost as far as Birmingham. Look west, and Wales beckons – on a clear day it might be possible to spot Snowdonia, and Cadair Idris.

Start/parking: Open area of verge

Satnav: SY7 9DU (nearest)	**Start GR:** SO 572850	**High Point GR:** SO 593865
OS Map: Landranger 138 Kidderminster & Wyre Forest		
Distance: 9km	**Ascent:** 270m	**Time:** 4hrs

Cafe/Pub: A good tea can be had in the locally renowned De Grey's cafe, which is in a beautiful timbered building in Ludlow and dates back to 1570 (01584 872764, www.degreys.co.uk).

Directions

Start from a big open area of verge by the minor road 1km west of Cockshutford. This is 1km north-east of Clee St Margaret at a point where four footpaths intersect.

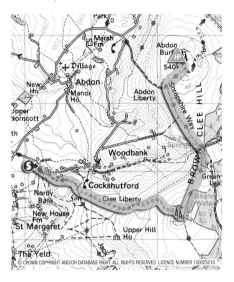

Follow the road SE for 200m, then take the fork in the road which leads through a gate, and goes along the N side of Nordy Bank fort. Continue along this towards the quarry at Clee Burf. 400m before the radio masts at Clee Burf, head NE and go for 800m across grassy ground to the Shropshire Way which goes along the brow of the hill at Green Lea; there is a footpath marked on the map but it is hard to find from this direction (but easy from the other!). Follow the Shropshire Way N then NW for 1.5km, until it crosses a footpath leading NE up to Abdon Burf. Follow this path for 500m up Brown Clee Hill to the summit at Abdon Burf. The top is marked by a viewing plinth. Immediately nearby is a large radio mast.

Nearby

A bonus in climbing this high point is being able to visit nearby Ludlow. Often referred to (with good reason) as the loveliest of all Britain's towns, it has nearly 500 listed buildings and a very buoyant foody culture – so much so that I was able to buy half a dozen jars of local honey in Ludlow itself. One mark of a thriving town (I discovered during my various trips) is the number of small independent shops they contain – greengrocers, butchers, bakers, ironmongers and the like. Ludlow scores five stars on this crude, but I think accurate, measure.

▲ LOOKING WEST FROM BROWN CLEE HILL

Dunkery Beacon_#55

519m | 1,703ft   30th | 14/10/08 | solo

A county of rolling hills, woodland and open fields, Somerset stretches south-west from Bristol to Devon. In the north, the county contains the city of Bath, with its Roman buildings and Royal Crescent; the Cheddar Gorge, where the oldest complete human skeleton was found; and Glastonbury, home to the famous festival and to Avalon – supposed burial place of King Arthur. Further south and west, the county contains several AONBs and national parks – the Mendip Hills, the Quantocks and Exmoor.

Somerset has long attracted authors and writers. Exmoor is, famously, *Lorna Doone* country, with real events and places incorporated into the novel. Jane Austen set many of her novels in Bath and Wordsworth and Coleridge lived for a time along the coast of northern Somerset, in villages such as Nether Stowey and Porlock. Travel through its green countryside, explore its characterful villages and enjoy its dramatic coastline, and it's easy to see what drew them here.

Dunkery Beacon, the high point, is the summit mound of Dunkery Hill in Exmoor, close to the coast. Topped by a huge cairn, it looks north across the Bristol Channel to Wales and south across the rolling countryside towards Devon. The lower flanks of the hill are wooded combes and green grass – typical of Exmoor in general – while the summit is surrounded by heathery, heathy moorland which breaks out into a deep purple colour in late summer.

Exmoor National Park contains over 700 square kilometres of rolling hills, wooded valleys and rocky coastline. It is a particularly beautiful place. The rugged coastline contains some of the highest sea cliffs in England, the hills feel particularly verdant and the villages, with their thatched cottages and covered markets, are some of the prettiest in the country. Look out for the wild ponies while you're there – these are Exmoor Ponies, the oldest native breed of horses in the UK.

Start/parking: Car park on Dunkery Hill

Satnav: PORLOCK (nearest)   **Start GR:** SS 904420   **High Point GR:** SS 891415

OS Map: Landranger 181 Minehead & Brendon Hills

Distance: 2.5km   **Ascent:** 80m   **Time:** 1.5hrs

Cafe/Pub: Porlock, beneath Dunkery Hill, has a choice of cafes and pubs. Try the Ship Inn (01643 862507, www.shipinnporlock.co.uk).

Directions

Start from the car park on Dunkery Hill next to the Kit Barrows cairns. This is on the minor road from Wheddon Cross to Porlock.

Follow the track SW then WSW for 1.2km to Dunkery Beacon, which has panoramic views north to Wales. The top is a huge cairn.

Nearby

Dunkery Beacon lies on the Macmillan Way, which runs to Lincolnshire. Why not wander along this for a short way? Or visit Porlock, a delightful village at the base of Dunkery Hill – together with Porlock Hill and Porlock beach. Further afield, visit the pretty cathedral city of Wells, Glastonbury Tor (from which there are lovely 360-degree views for miles) and the delightful city of Bath. And track down the exceptionally tasty, multi-award winning Montgomery cheddar cheese.

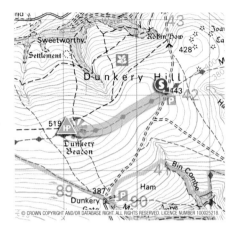

▲ THE CAIRN MARKING THE TOP OF DUNKERY BEACON

▲ THE PATH WEST OVER EXMOOR FROM DUNKERY BEACON

Staffordshire

Cheeks Hill_#54

520m | 1,706ft   23ʳᵈ | 22/08/08 | solo

Staffordshire lies in the West Midlands, between Manchester and Birmingham. Within its borders lies some beautiful countryside: part of the Peak District National Park and the AONB of Cannock Chase; some significant transport links – a stretch of the M6, the longest motorway in Britain, and more canals than in any other county in England; and several major towns and small cities.

 The county town of Staffordshire, Stoke-on-Trent, is recognised as the pottery centre of the UK. The area, sometimes known as 'The Potteries', rose to this position in the 17th century, when men such as Josiah Wedgewood took the industry to an industrial scale. This was partly due to the local availability of raw materials, such as clay, salt, lead and coal, and partly thanks to ever-improving transport links to the region. Waterways such as the Trent and Mersey Canal were a considerable improvement over bumpy horse-drawn carts for the transportation of fragile goods!

 Cheeks Hill lies in the north of Staffordshire, on Axe Edge Moor in the very south-west corner of the Peak District. It is one of the wilder corners of that national park, featuring large areas of open, featureless ground and high moorland. The hilltop is crossed by a drystone wall, which marks the boundary between Staffordshire and Derbyshire, and is only a mile or so away from Three Shire Heads – a point in a shallow river valley, near a stone packhorse bridge, where the two counties also meet Cheshire.

 The high point is unusual in that it is on the side of a hill rather than the top (the higher points are in Derbyshire). It requires rather fiddly map reading to cross the grass heathland and find the high point, which I designated as a post in the ground.

Start/parking: Road near Dane Head

Satnav: BUXTON (nearest)	**Start GR:** SK 030702	**High Point GR:** SK 026700
OS Map: Landranger 119 Buxton & Matlock		
Distance: 2km	**Ascent:** 40m	**Time:** 1hr
Cafe/Pub: Nearby Buxton has many tearooms and dinner options.		

Directions

Start near Dane Head on the verge of the minor road which leads NW to SE across Axe Edge Moor, 5km SW of Buxton.

Follow SW for 700m the national trail which crosses the road 200m east of Dane Head. Near a disused mineshaft, the trail meets another path; turn NNE and follow this path for 300m until it meets the intersection of two fences. This is the Staffordshire high point, on the side but not the top of Cheeks Hill, and is unmarked. The route is tricky to follow as there are more paths on the ground than are marked on the map!

Nearby

The village of Flash, three kilometres away, is, at 1,518 feet, the highest village in Britain. A short distance further is the spa town of Buxton, with a range of cafes and fine pubs, opera house, caves and, of course, spas: www.visitbuxton.co.uk. The Wedgewood museum in Barlaston is also interesting.

▲ THE STAFFORDSHIRE HIGH POINT, ON THE SIDE OF CHEEKS HILL

▲ AXE EDGE MOOR AROUND CHEEKS HILL

Ben Lomond_#11

974m | 3,196ft   3rd | May 2004 | with Harry aged 13

The city of Stirling is known as the 'Gateway to the Highlands'. Sitting on the geographical Highland Boundary Fault that separates the Scottish Highlands from the Lowlands, it was once of strategic importance in Scotland, and formerly the capital of the country. Nowadays, the A9 – a major route into to the Highlands – begins just north of the city, meaning that many north-bound travellers still pass through the 'gateway'.

Thanks to its strategic location, the county was the site of many historic battles in years gone by. The Battle of Bannockburn, one of the key moments in Scottish history and a significant victory over the English, was fought near Stirling, and William Wallace – one of the main leaders of the Scottish Wars of Independence (and of *Braveheart* fame) – was defeated in the Battle of Falkirk, in south Stirlingshire.

The county top is Ben Lomond, a distinctive mountain in a wonderful spot, overlooking Loch Lomond. At 3,196 feet tall, it earns a spot on the list of Munros (a Scottish mountain over 3,000 feet) and, being close to Glasgow and easily accessible, is one of the more popular on that list. It sits in the beautiful Loch Lomond and The Trossachs National Park. A craggy, rocky mountain, it is formed by the meeting of two south-facing ridges – the roughly conical summit rising from the point where they meet. I climbed the mountain with Harry when he was thirteen, as a 'dry run' before tackling Ben Nevis. The ascent is quite a slog – we climbed through mist and rain – but rewards success with superb views across Loch Lomond and the mountains beyond. Harry (but not I!) celebrated our success with a bracing swim in Loch Lomond afterwards, which was a lot of fun.

Start/parking: Car park near Rowardennan Hotel

Satnav: G63 0AR   **Start GR:** NS 360983   **High Point GR:** NN 366028

OS Map: Landranger 56 Loch Lomond & Inverary

Distance: 11km   **Ascent:** 940m   Time: 7.5hrs

Cafe/Pub: A pleasant pint is available on tap at the Clansman bar in the Rowardennan Hotel (01360 870273).

Directions

Start at Rowardennan Hotel. Follow the path from the hotel NE through the woods; it emerges to open country after 1km. Then follow the path up the crest of the hill NE, then N, then NNW for 4km to the summit of Ben Lomond. The top is a trig point.

Return via Ptarmigan. Take the path W from the summit down to Bealach Buidhe. Then go SW and then S past the east side of some little lochans to Ptarmigan, which is 1.5km from the Ben Lomond summit. There are lovely views west over Loch Lomond and beyond. Follow the track for 4km SSE then S back down to Rowardennan.

Nearby

On our drive back to Glasgow from Ben Lomond, we unfortunately got a bit lost, but were lucky enough to happen on the Glengoyne distillery – this was very appealing as Glengoyne is my favourite whisky! Lying a little way from the southern end of Loch Lomond, it is well worth a visit. www.glengoyne.com

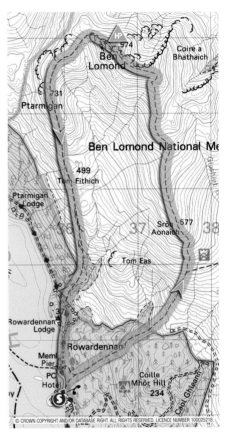

▲ HARRY AT THE TOP OF BEN LOMOND

▲ BEN LOMOND FROM PTARMIGAN

Great Wood_ #84

128m | 420ft   7ᵗʰ | 13/06/08 | with Alex

The county of Suffolk dates back to the fifth century, to the time of the Angles, after whom East Anglia and England itself are named. The name refers to the 'south folk' in that region. Partnering Norfolk (or 'north folk') on the east coast of England, Suffolk is every bit as flat as its northern neighbour. It is a low-lying, very open county – the eighth largest county in Britain by area, but only thirty-second in population, with most of its inhabitants living in small villages in rural farming areas.

Suffolk is famed for the charm of its buildings and the beauty of its countryside – it contains two significant areas of natural beauty: the Suffolk Broads in the north, and the Suffolk Coast and Heaths, which for me is the best part. The Suffolk Broads are part of 'the Broads' (see Norfolk, p172) a large area of wetland in the north of the county. The coast and heaths, meanwhile, are a designated AONB, covering well over a hundred square miles of wetlands, heathlands and shingle beaches. There are three RSPB nature reserves in the area, protecting a wonderful area of tranquil and unspoilt landscape.

Great Wood lies south-west from Bury St Edmonds – although to describe it as a 'hill' would be stretching things somewhat, as the countryside is pretty flat. It is the highest part of the Newmarket Ridge, a 20-mile long line of low (!) hills which start near Bishop's Stortford in Hertfordshire and end near Great Wood. The top is a radio mast right next to the road in the woods, reached via a short walk. No one else was there.

Start/parking: Road junction south of Depden

Satnav: IP29 4BU	**Start GR:** TL 781564	**High Point GR:** TL 787558
OS Map: Landranger 155 Bury St Edmunds		
Distance: 2km	**Ascent:** 20m	**Time:** 0.5hrs

Cafe/Pub: Continue south over the hill to the village of Rede, to visit the Plough Inn and make a nice extension to the walk (01284 789208). Alternatively, there are several cafes in nearby Bury St Edmunds.

Directions

Start 1km south of Depden, which is 10km SW down the A143 from Bury St Edmunds.

Follow the minor road SW from the A143 for 700m, past Elms Farm to the radio mast in the woods ahead. This mast marks the top.

Nearby

Pop in to Bury St Edmunds and visit The Nutshell – Britain's smallest pub. Measuring just fifteen by seven feet, they have, apparently, managed to cram 102 people into its bar. If you're lucky, they'll have the local Adnams (from Southwold) and Greene King (from Bury St Edmunds) on tap, as these beers are a treat. Further afield, visit the nice little towns of Aldeburgh (home of the Aldeburgh Music Festival) and Southwold, or walk the pebble beaches and visit the nature reserves around Orford Ness.

▲ THE GREAT WOOD

Surrey

Leith Hill_#65

295m | 968ft   19th | 13/08/08 | solo

One of the busiest and most densely populated counties in the country, visitors to Surrey are often surprised by how green the county is. Despite being on London's doorstep, and thus full of commuters, it is very easy to find peace and quiet in Surrey's leafy woodlands.

Small woodlands and green fields line the roadsides as you travel between towns. Sandy heathlands lie on the outskirts of villages and, towards the south of the county, are the Surrey Hills. These are a series of wooded hills which form part of the North Downs and cover a quarter of Surrey. They are formed by a chalk and sandstone ridge which runs into Kent (the North Downs continue down towards the White Cliffs of Dover). Walking through them, it's hard to believe the proximity to London and the M25.

The county top, Leith Hill, is in the Surrey Hills. It is, at 968 feet, the second highest point in South East England. (Depending on your definition of South East, it may be considered the highest – only Walbury Hill, at the western end of Berkshire, is higher.) The top is marked by an 18th century tower (almost a folly). The 64-foot height of the tower pushes the hill just above the 1,000-foot level, from where some say it is possible to see into 13 counties. Many people are content, as I was, to buy a piece of cake from the shop in its base.

There have been many interesting occurrences over the years. Surrey is where the Magna Carta was sealed in 1215, at Runnymede. The world's first motor-racing circuit was built here, at Brooklands near Woking in 1907, and sections of its huge banked concrete corners can still be seen. Horsell Common, also near Woking and a pleasant place for a gentle stroll, was the site of the Martian landing in H. G. Wells' *War of the Worlds* and Epsom Racecourse – home to the prestigious Derby, one of the world's premier horse-racing events – lies in the west of the county.

Start/parking: Car park south of Leith Hill

Satnav: RH5 6LX	**Start GR:** TQ 139428	**High Point GR:** TQ 139431

OS Map: Landranger 187 Dorking & Reigate

Distance: 1km	**Ascent:** 70m	**Time:** 0.5hrs

Cafe/Pub: There is a small 'hatch' in Leith Hill tower, selling home-made cakes and other snacks. Otherwise, the Plough Inn in Coldharbour is a short distance away and there are good pubs in virtually every local village.

Directions

Start from the car park just south of Leith Hill on the minor road 1km SW of Coldharbour, which is 5km S of Dorking.

Follow the track N for 300m up to the tower, which marks the top of Leith Hill.

Nearby

Just west of Leith Hill is Holmbury Hill. Park in the pretty village of Holmbury St Mary and climb to the top for some incredible views out south towards the English Channel. Other good places to visit include the RHS gardens at Wisley, Box Hill, Polesden Lacey and the Epsom racecourse.

▲ LEITH HILL TOWER

BY: ISTOCK

Sussex

Black Down_#67

280m | 919ft   18th | 13/08/08 | solo

Relatively heavily developed along the seafront, with a number of towns and cities (Eastbourne, Brighton, Worthing and Chichester, for example), Sussex becomes more rural as you move inland. Immediately north of the towns are the South Downs – which became, in 2011, a national park. The Downs are a large area of chalk downland; rolling hills covered in scrubby grass, bushes and trees and fields of yellow corn, often dotted with red poppies. This colourful landscape of greens, yellows and whites is frequently set against a clear blue sky, giving the Downs (in certain months) a truly summer feel.

Further north is the Sussex Weald. Lying between the North and South Downs, this was once a heavily wooded area ('weald' is derived from the Old English word for 'forest'), but is now predominantly flat and open, although it is still dotted with pockets of ancient woodland and Sussex remains one of the most heavily-wooded counties in the UK.

The county top, Black Down, is in the South Downs. One of the highest hills in South East England and the highest point in the national park, it is a wild and peaceful landscape of long grass, pine trees and heather. The top itself – a trig point – is in woodland and it can be quite hard to find, hidden in the undergrowth, away from any footpath and on quite flat ground.

I visited Black Down only a couple of months after beginning my *High Point* project. Searching for the top amongst the trees was an amusing forerunner to many of the somewhat unusual high point sites I would come across later on and to an extent energised me to continue the project – clearly I was going to be coming across some unusual spots. That aside, Black Down had a rather spooky feel to it, which I find is quite often the case in woods and forests (maybe I shouldn't have watched the *Blair Witch Project* or *Deliverance* films ...) so I was glad to finish the walk.

Start/parking: Car park

Satnav: GU27 3BS (nearest)	**Start GR:** SU 922290	**High Point GR:** SU 919296
OS Map: Landranger 197 Chichester & the South Downs		
Distance: 1.5km	**Ascent:** 90m	**Time:** 1hr
Cafe/Pub: Haslemere, five kilometres away, has various cafes, shops and pubs.		

Directions

Start from the small car park on the minor road 5km south-east of Haslemere, just north of Blackdown Farm and south of Abesters.

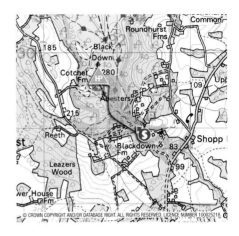

Follow the track NW for 300m up to the Temple of the Winds viewpoint. Take the track N for 300m and then seek out the summit just W of here. This can be tricky as the summit plateau is flat and heavily wooded, and there is no real footpath to the top. The top is a trig point.

Nearby

Walk the South Downs Way, which you can join about ten miles to the south of Black Down and which runs the length of the South Downs National Park. Further afield you can visit the fascinating Hastings Fishermen's Museum, next to the unique net sheds (fifty tall, black wooden sheds used to dry fishing gear) on Hastings old town's beach. Also visit the site of the 1066 Battle of Hastings at (appropriately-named) Battle, and Rye, a characterful town and old Cinque Port.

▲ THE SUSSEX HIGH POINT, ON BLACK DOWN

Ben More Assynt (Beinn Mhòr Asaint)_#9

998m | 3,274ft   52nd | 13/08/09 | solo

Sutherland stretches across the north coast of Scotland. Now officially in the Highlands, it is the fifth-largest Scottish county in terms of area, but has a mere 13,000 people living within its borders – less than most small towns.

This is due in part to the Highland Clearances of the 18th and 19th centuries, when forcible evictions were carried out across the Highlands during an agricultural revolution to make way for large-scale sheep-based farming and trade. This, combined with crop failures, saw tens of thousands (including some of my wife's ancestors) leave the Highlands – some travelling as far as Canada. Sutherland was particularly badly affected.

Another reason for the low population is the spectacularly rugged landscape. Vast areas of mountainous land with few roads and no settlements dominate the centre of the county. The few towns that exist are dotted around the edges, like Dornoch, the county town on the east coast. (Even Dornoch has a population of under 2,000!)

The county top, Ben More Assynt, is a memorable mountain. It lies in the Assynt 'geopark', probably the most surprising and genuinely awesome area in Britain, where mountains such as Suilven and Canisp soar strangely, and almost alarmingly, into the sky above a beautiful landscape of remarkable rock features. In the context of the bizarre Assynt area, Ben More Assynt is surprisingly normal (not dissimilar to what you might find else-where in the Highlands). The walk to the top is straightforward until its final part, where it becomes tricky as it crosses sharp boulders in the final stretch to the summit. The views from the top were stunning and I could even see the Morayshire coastline in the distance, over fifty miles away. I came across just five people – and two eagles – on my walk.

My trip was made extra special as Ben More Assynt was just ten miles away from the Ledbeg farm and Aulannakalgach (now Altnacealgach) house (now Inn) where Alex's Macleod ancestors had lived some 200 years ago. All of Assynt therefore was for us seemingly full of ghosts and it was fascinating to visit these properties and find out about the times they lived in – these would have been tough in any case but were undoubtedly made worse by the Highland Clearances going on at the time.

Start/parking: Car park at Inchnadamph

Satnav: IV27 4HN	Start GR: NC 250216	High Point GR: NC 318201
OS Map: Landranger 15 Loch Assynt		
Distance: 18km	Ascent: 1,130m	Time: 10hrs

Cafe/Pub: Approximately eleven kilometres north, on the A894, is a nice little cafe in the tiny Maryck Memories of Childhood museum just before Unapool.

Directions

Start from the car park at Inchnadamph, just off the A837, at the southern end of Loch Assynt. If possible, arrive in Assynt via the A832 coast road driving north from Torridon – the views are just stunning.

Cross the bridge over River Traligill and turn E immediately along a track which goes to the right of a large hostel. Follow the track, which stays north of River Traligill, E then SE past Glenbain and along Gleann Dubh. The track reverts to E and then turns to NE when it goes steeply up Allt a Choinne Mhill. There are many moraines when the track levels out; then it rises up (still NE) steeply to a lochan which is 5km from the start. Go SSE and steeply up for 1.5km to the munro Conival. Then head E for 1.5km, steeply down and then up, to reach Ben More Assynt – this stretch is demanding as the route crosses big sharp boulders which can be slippery and difficult if wet. The top is a rocky outcrop with panoramic views.

Nearby

Browse the stunning, other-worldly scenery, particularly Suilven, Canisp and Stac Pollaidh. Visit the Highland Stoneware pottery in Lochinver – this was interesting to visit as I have eaten off their plates and bowls at home for some thirty years! Walk the seafront at Ullapool. Drive alongside the remote Loch Shin. Generally, soak up the wilderness which is all around in Sutherland.

▲ BEN MORE ASSYNT FROM CONIVAL

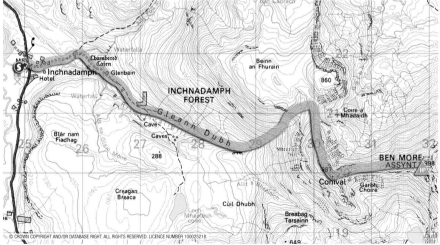

© CROWN COPYRIGHT AND/OR DATABASE RIGHT. ALL RIGHTS RESERVED. LICENCE NUMBER 100025218.

▲ LOOKING SOUTH-WEST FROM BEN MORE ASSYNT TOWARDS CANISP AND SUILVEN

Warwickshire

Ebrington Hill_#71

261m | 856ft   37ᵗʰ | 20/03/09 | with Alex

Several places in England claim to be in the dead centre of the country – and Warwickshire can claim two of them. One is Meriden, in the south-west of the county, where a medieval stone pillar marks the 'traditional centre of England'. Another contender is the Midland Oak, in Leamington Spa in the centre of Warwickshire, on the spot exactly halfway up and halfway across England. It's not the original oak, of course, but one planted from a locally-found acorn to replace the one before it (and so on). The Ordnance Survey disagrees with both claims, naming Lindley Hall Farm in neighbouring Leicestershire as the true centre (see p150).

But even if Leicestershire does officially claim the centre point, Warwickshire is rightly famous for several other reasons. It is, as road signs proudly declare on the way in, 'Shakespeare's County' – the playwright was born in Stratford-upon-Avon. Authors George Elliot, Rupert Brooke and Philip Larkin were also born here. In sports, it was in the north of the county in 1823 that a schoolboy named William Webb Ellis picked up a ball and ran with it – at Rugby School – marking the point at which the eponymous game is said to have begun. And in engineering, it was in Coventry at the end of the 18th century that the British motor industry started with the production of the first Coventry Daimler. Since then, Rover, Hillman, Jaguar, Healey have all worked in the area. Triumph even had a factory near the centre point at Meriden.

The county top is Ebrington Hill. An unremarkable high point, it is a little more than a trig point in a wall amongst open fields, near to some radio masts. It does, however, lie just east of the excellent gardens at Hidcote Manor, and north east of the lovely Cotswold stone village of Chipping Camden – so there's plenty to see in the area, even if the high point disappoints!

Start/parking: Radio masts

Satnav: GL55 6LR (Hidcote Manor, nearby)   **Start GR:** SP 187426   **High Point GR:** SP 186427

OS Map: Landranger 151 Stratford-upon-Avon

Distance: 0.5km   **Ascent:** 0m   **Time:** 0.5hrs

Cafe/Pub: Good tea and cakes at the Bantam tearooms in nearby Chipping Camden, where you can also buy Warwickshire honey with a picture of Shakespeare's head on the label. (01386 840386, www.bantamtea-rooms.co.uk). The Ebrington Arms in nearby Ebrington is a good gastropub. (01386 593 223, www.theebringtonarms.co.uk).

Directions

Start near the radio masts on the verge of the minor road running NNE 1km E of Hidcote Manor.

Follow the track W towards Hidcote for 100m. Just past the radio masts, head N along the W side of a stone wall to the trig point. There is a large flat summit plateau, and the trig point is commonly designated as the top.

An alternative, and better, route (if you are visiting Hidcote Gardens) is to park in the car park of Hidcote Manor. Then follow the restricted byway ESE for 700m from the middle of the car park up to the radio masts; the path zigzags right then left halfway up. Then head N alongside the stone wall to the trig point.

Nearby

Visit the splendid garden at Hidcote Manor – a beautiful 'arts and crafts' garden in the north Cotswolds (www.nationaltrust.org.uk/hidcote), and the small town of Chipping Camden, which is one of the most picturesque villages in the Cotswolds. Further afield are the hugely attractive villages of Bourton-on-the-Water, Stow-on-the-Wold, and Moreton-in-Marsh – all having lovely golden Cotswold stone buildings and Stratford-upon-Avon, Shakespeare's birthplace, full of historic black and white buildings.

▲ THE TOP OF EBRINGTON HILL

West Cairn Hill_#45

562m | 1,841ft   59th | 04/03/10 | with Charlie

Known as Linlithgowshire until 1921, West Lothian is a small county just west of Edinburgh. Only the 20th largest out of 32 Scottish counties, it is densely populated (the ninth biggest) due to its proximity to the capital. Despite this, it contains some beautiful rolling countryside if you wish to get away from the towns.

The county top, West Cairn Hill, is in one such area: the Pentland Hills. These are a small range of hills, some 20 miles long and never more than 580 metres high, which run south-west from Edinburgh towards the central Scottish Borders. Despite being one of the lowest of Scotland's county high points, the walk turned out to be one my toughest, on account of a deep covering of snow.

This walk was a memorable one. It was with some trepidation that my future son-in-law Charlie and I set out. The air was thick with mist and the ground covered with snow. We knew we could only reach the top if the weather improved, as it had been forecast to do and as, after about a kilometre, it duly did. Now under a lovely blue sky, we walked on, gaining height along the (concealed by snow, but in any case pretty indistinct) Thieves Road as far as Cauldstane Slap before turning west up the broad ridge towards our summit. The snow eased in places, but deepened in others and, before long, we found the snow deeper than ever – above knee level on occasion. I normally try to avoid walking in snow, and it was seriously hard work to reach the top, but we were superbly rewarded when we got there. Anybody who has walked in, or even seen, the Scottish hills under a covering a snow will be able to imagine the magical Winter Wonderland scene around us – a shining landscape of clean, white hills sparkling under a lovely blue sky. It's the sort of view you can never see too often.

Start/parking: Car park at Little Vantage		
Satnav: EH27 8DJ (closest)	**Start GR:** NT 101628	**High Point GR:** NT 107584
OS Map: Landranger 72 Upper Clyde Valley		
Distance: 11km	**Ascent:** 410m	**Time:** 5hrs
Cafe/Pub: There's nowhere particularly close – head north a few miles to Linlithgow or Livingston.		

Directions

Start from the car park at Little Vantage on the A70, 1km north of Harperrig Reservoir.

Follow the track signposted *Cauldstane Slap* SSE for 2km, initially alongside a wall, past Gala Ford and the east side of Harperrig. Continue SSE for 2km along the old Thieves Road track up to Cauldstane Slap, which is roughly midway between East Cairn Hill and West Cairn Hill. Follow the wall SW then WNW for 1.2km up to the summit of West Cairn Hill. The top is a trig point.

Nearby

It's worth making a trip north to Linlithgow. A historic town, its impressive castle was the birthplace of Mary Queen of Scots, the loch near its centre is a highly popular site and it has a fine medieval church.

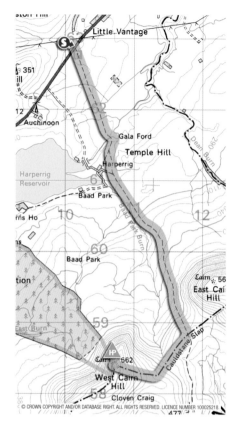

▲ WEST CAIRN HILL

▲ THE WINTER WONDERLAND FROM WEST CAIRN HILL

An Cliseam_#25

799m | 2,621ft   84ᵗʰ | 19/06/11 | solo

The Western Isles – or Outer Hebrides – are not a historic county. Split instead between Inverness- and Ross-shires, they are part of the Highlands and Islands region. However, any high point project would seem incomplete without a trip to the Isles, and it is for that reason that they are included here.

    The Isles consist of Lewis and Harris, North and South Uist, Benbecula and Barra, collectively stretching for over 100 stunning miles along the north-west coast of Scotland. There's a surprising variety in the landscape, from the rocky mountains of Harris to the flatter, moorland-covered Lewis. Some of the most impressive beaches in Britain are found on the coasts, with clean sandy shores and stunningly clear waters. The air, blowing in from the sea, is equally clear, allowing you to pick out remarkable levels of detail on far-off hillsides.

    The highest point is An Cliseam (also known as Clisham) on Harris, which seems to be (rightly!) regarded by all who visit it as a special place. Only a couple of miles from the road, my walk (on my birthday) was surprisingly tough – I failed to find the path (although I subsequently found it on the way back down), which resulted in me having to scramble across a lot of slippery (in the wet) boulders on a very steep ascent. The final section is narrow and felt exposed in the wind and cloud. The top (a trig point) was fun to discover as, being surrounded by a circular wall of stones, it is invisible until you are right next to it.

    Having now visited three times, the Western Isles conjure up countless lovely memories and images: the vistas, the beaches (Scarista, Luskentyre), the coastal machair, the sunsets, the Harris tweed, the 12th-century Isle of Lewis chessmen (which I saw in Stornaway), the crofts, the Callanish stones, Effie Galletly's quilts of Hebridean scenes, the 'Lochmaddy' carrot cake, fresh langoustines, the Old Tom Morris golf course at Askernish, Scarista House (my favourite hotel in all of Britain), and the world immortalised by Mairi Hedderwick's drawings, Compton Mackenzie's *Whisky Galore* and Finlay MacDonald's *Crowdie and Cream* ... even the Akram General Stores in Tarbert; if you need almost any household item (vases, hair dryers, boots, light bulbs – you name it), they will probably have it in stock!

Start/parking: Car park on A859

Satnav: HS3 3AG (nearest)   **Start GR:** NB 174057   **High Point GR:** NB 154073

OS Map: Landranger 13 West Lewis & North Harris; Landranger 14 Tarbert & Loch Seaforth

Distance: 4km   **Ascent:** 660m   **Time:** 4.5hrs

Cafe/Pub: Tea is available at the Harris Hotel in nearby Tarbert (01859 502154, www.harrishotel.com). Approximately 15 kilometres south-west of Tarbert, there is superb dinner and accommodation at the lovely Scarista House in Scarista.

Directions

Start from the first of the car parks on the A859 approximately 9km from Tarbert. This car park is at the point where the road crosses the Abhainn Mharaig stream, just past Sron Carsacleit.

Follow the path NW alongside the stream. When after 400m the stream forks into two tributaries, follow a route which goes midway between the two and directly towards An Cliseam. The path is quite indistinct and easy to miss in the early part of the route. Approx 1km from the fork, and just as the route gets very steep, the path reforms and becomes clear; this leads directly to the An Cliseam summit. The final section is quite narrow and feels somewhat exposed particularly if windy (which is likely!), as some (quite easy) scrambling over rocks is required. The top is a trig point surrounded by a circular wall of stones, which shields the trig point until you are right next to it.

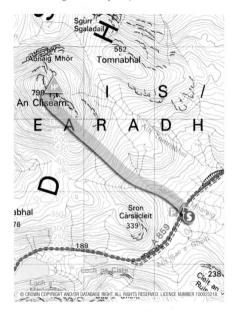

Return by retracing your steps.

Note that the route is more hazardous than it seems when viewed from the start. Firstly, you may be tempted (as I was) to head alongside the stream to the bealach between An Cliseam and Sron Carsacleit, and then to go NNW up An Cliseam. There is no path up this route and much scrambling over boulders on the steep sections – care is needed as they are quite slippy in the wet. Secondly, do not stray onto the E face of An Cliseam, as it is very steep and rocky.

▲ LOOKING DOWN TOWARDS THE STARTING POINT

Nearby

Visit the lovely beaches at Huisinis (at the end of the B887 going north westwards), Luskentyre (which has views across to Taransay, where BBC's *Castaway 2000* was filmed) and Scarista.

▲ THE SUMMIT OF AN CLISEAM

Helvellyn_#12

950m | 3,117ft   2nd | 15/06/10 (and 1974) | with Tim and Anne

Westmorland's county boundaries run along Windermere in the west, up and over the county top of Helvellyn and along Ullswater in the north. In the south, they run down towards Morecombe Bay and cross to the Yorkshire Dales National Park in the east. This is a beautiful county containing some of England's best-loved countryside. Parts of the Howgills and the Eden Valley, the Lakeland valleys of Troutbeck and Kentmere and the popular shores of Windermere all fall within its boundaries.

One particularly popular spot is the county top – Helvellyn. The third highest mountain in England, it overlooks Ullswater, which is perhaps modern-day Cumbria's most beautiful lake. Formed from a long ridge between Patterdale and Thirlmere, it is most often climbed on its dramatic east side. Here, sharp ridges between large cliffs wind precariously up towards the summit, an open plateau of stone and short grass sloping gently away to the west. So flat is the plateau that, in 1926, a plane managed to land and take off there.

My route climbed very steeply out of Glenridding, following a stony track up to the wonderfully-named Hole-in-the-Wall, from which the quiet, sheltered waters of Red Tarn can be seen far below. The route then follows Striding Edge to the summit. This is quite exposed and, depending on the route you choose, you may need to use your hands in places.

I had climbed Helvellyn thirty-six years previously in 1974 – too long ago to qualify as part of my *High Point* project, so I repeated the climb with my brother Tim and his wife Anne. In many ways, the best part of the route was the return via Nethermost and Dollywagon Pikes and Grisedale, which are lovely and far less popular than the more touristy routes. I saw a superb range of wildlife around my base at Grassthwaite Howe – red squirrel, fox, pheasant, rabbit, badger, weasel, woodpecker and dozens of different types of birds. It was easy to see how the Lake District must have fed Beatrix Potter with her ideas.

Start/parking: Glenridding car park

Satnav: CA11 0PD	**Start GR:** NY 386169	**High Point GR:** NY 341151
OS Map: Landranger 90 Penrith & Keswick		
Distance: 14km	**Ascent:** 800m	**Time:** 7.5hrs
Cafe/Pub: There are several good pubs and cafes to choose from in Glenridding.		

Nearby

For another day's walking, climb the steep and grassy High Street from Hartsop, or take the Ullswater ferry from Glenridding across to Howtown, and wander back around the side of the lake. For something more sedate, visit Ambleside, a pleasant Lakeland town from which you can take a cruise on Lake Windermere, or visit the interesting Arts & Crafts Blackwell House near Bowness; generally, just soak up the amazing Lake District scenery.

Directions

Start from the car park at Glenridding.

Follow the road along the south side of Glenridding Beck for 400m and then take the track S past Westside for 500m to Lanty's Tarn. Continue for 300m until reaching the track which goes WSW, 200m from Grassthwaite Howe. Follow this past Brownend Plantation and then W upwards for 2km until reaching the ridge at Hole-in-the-Wall, from where you can see Red Tarn below. Continue upwards WSW then W for 2km across Striding Edge, which is quite exposed and you may need to use your hands in places, and up to the Helvellyn summit. The top is a trig point.

Return by going S for 3km along the ridge to Nethermost Pike, to Dollywagon Pike and down to Grisedale Tarn. Then take the track NE for 4km down Grisedale back to the point just below Lanty's Tarn. Then return to Glenridding, following the ascent route. This route down Helvellyn is quite straightforward and has lovely views.

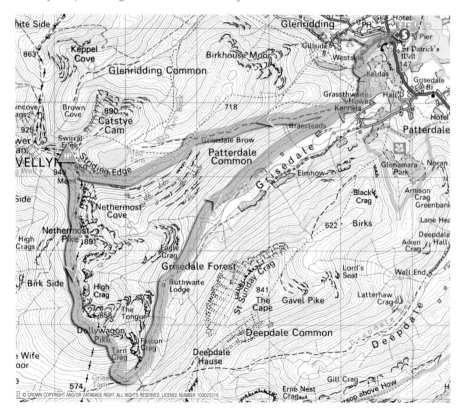

▲ LOOKING DOWN GRISEDALE TOWARDS ULLSWATER FROM NETHERMOST PIKE

Craig Airie Fell_#62

322m | 1,056ft   47th | 17/07/09 | with Alex

Wigtownshire is one of those counties which few people seem to be aware of. It was formerly the most south-westerly county in Scotland, jutting out into the Irish Sea and the Solway Firth. Bordered to the east by Kirkcudbrightshire, the two counties jointly form the region of Galloway and are an area of great natural beauty.

Much of the area is countryside, with the majority of towns and settlements lying on the coast. For some reason, the sky here seems immense, a real 'big sky'. Much of the inland area is forested, and, for Scotland, relatively low, but still with a very remote feel. Toward the coast is the Machars region, a peninsula of rolling land (the name means 'low-lying'), and a mixture of sandy beaches and rocky coastline, while inland are green hills and peaty moorland. The region has a mild climate, (particularly for Scotland!), with many plants more commonly associated with warmer areas thriving, and the coast occasionally being visited by basking sharks and dolphins.

Wigtownshire lies to the east of the Machars (the largest town in the area is the port of Stranraer, some way west) – a pretty little town of about 1,000 people that is Scotland's National Book Town and well worth a trip.

The county top, Craig Airie Fell, sits further north, inland, about 15 miles east of Stranraer on the Southern Upland Way (a 212-mile coast-to-coast footpath across Scotland, which starts in nearby Portpatrick). The peak is in an area of rather uninteresting marshy scrubland and forest, but, being a hundred feet or so higher than the surrounding terrain, has an impressive vista of views for miles around.

Start/parking: On minor road

Satnav: DG8 6RZ	Start GR: NX 270732	High Point GR: NX 236736
OS Map: Landranger 76 Girvan		
Distance: 8.5km	Ascent: 160m	Time: 3.5hrs

Cafe/Pub: Various options in nearby Newton Stewart.

Directions

Start approximately 1km W of Polbae on the verge of the minor road which is the Southern Upland Way. Polbae is in the forest 4km WNW of Knowe, which is on the B7027, 10km NW of Newton Stewart.

Follow the road past the end of the forest and continue past the N side of Derry farm, and then W past Loch Derry. 1.8km from Derry the track heads NW through the forest. Continue along this NW and then up to the top of Craig Airie Fell. The top is a trig point on open land above the forest. This is a remote spot, with extensive views in all directions.

Nearby

Visit the former county town of Wigtown, an interesting town in the pleasant Machars region of rolling green hills The town is designated Scotland's National Book Town and home to the annual Wigtown Book Festival: www.wigtown-booktown.co.uk

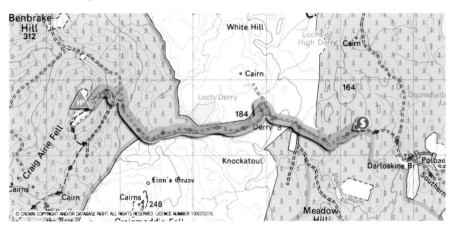

▲ ON TOP OF CRAIG AIRIE FELL

Wiltshire

Milk Hill_ #64

295m | 968ft   6th | 08/06/08 | with Alex

Milk Hill is a rather curious place. On its flanks lies the Alton white horse, the third largest in the county, with at least one other chalk horse visible from the hilltop. The exact reasons behind the creation of many of such horses is uncertain – though not as uncertain the crop circles which periodically appear in the farmland overlooked by Milk Hill. There were many there when I visited, some being of great complexity and strange beauty.

Until a few years ago, there was something of a dispute as to whether Milk Hill or nearby Tan Hill was Wiltshire's high point – but Milk Hill won out after some analysis on the BBC's *Countryfile* deemed it to be only ten inches higher. As a top, Milk Hill has a special significance for me in that it was the first high point which I tackled after starting my *High Point* project in earnest in June 2008. It was a good starting trip: a nice walk on a lovely day with splendid views in a part of the country which I had never explored before – the essence of the project.

The Hill is in the North Wessex Downs, a large open area of rolling grass and woodland that stretches west from Berkshire. Continue further south across the county, you encounter the vast Salisbury Plain, a massive area of chalk downland and huge open skies. It is well-known for its rich archaeology, containing the famous Stonehenge and Avebury stone circles, along with innumerable barrows, and tumuli. More recently, it has become known as the training ground for much of the British Military – including the 'lost' village of Imber, whose entire population was, in 1943, evicted to make way for American soldiers training to invade German and French villages. It's been shot to pieces on a regular basis ever since!

Wiltshire is a lovely county, full of interesting towns and villages. There is Salisbury, with its cathedral; Devizes, with its open market place and local beers and the delightful Castle Combe – home to the racecourse but also a very pretty village.

Start/parking: Car park at SU 115 637

Satnav: SN8 4LB (nearest)	**Start GR:** SU 115637	**High Point GR:** SU 104643

OS Map: Landranger 165 Aylesbury & Leighton Buzzard

Distance: 3.5km	**Ascent:** 80m	**Time:** 1.5hrs

Cafe/Pub: Try the Barge, half a mile away in Honeystreet (01672 851705, www.the-barge-inn.com). Alternatively, there are nice coffee and cakes at the Azuza Coffee Shop in nearby Hungerford.

Directions

Start from the car park 1.5km north along the minor road from Alton Barnes to Marlborough.

Cross the road and follow the track W then SW for 400m until it forks. Take the right fork WNW for 500m up to the white horse. Follow the track W then NE and N for 1km; then go E across a field for 300m to the top. The summit area is flat and the top is not obvious; it has been the subject of debate and arguably it is the spot marked by a small cairn.

Nearby

Visit the famous Caen Hill flight of twenty-nine locks on the Kennet and Avon Canal, near Devizes – an impressive sight! Or visit the Avebury Ring prehistoric stone circles, which are among the most impressive in the country. Whatever you do, don't miss a pint of the local Wadworth's beer, which comes from Devizes. Further afield, visit Stonehenge, a UNESCO World Heritage Site; or Salisbury Cathedral, which has the tallest church spire (404 feet) in Britain and an original copy of the Magna Carta.

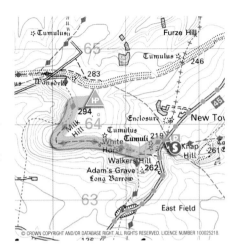

▲ THE WHITE HORSE ON MILK HILL

▲ LOOKING SOUTH FROM MILK HILL

Worcestershire Beacon_#59

425m | 1,394ft   4th | May 2006 | solo

Worcestershire lies in the West Midlands, its boundaries running north from the top of the Cotswolds towards Birmingham, and west towards Wales – and the Malvern Hills, where the high point is found. The green countryside and thick woodland in the county is thought to have been J. R. R. Tolkien's inspiration for the Hobbits' *Shire*, and also perhaps for *The Archers*: the fictional Ambridge is set in an imaginary county between Worcestershire and Warwickshire.

The Malvern Hills are a distinctive range running along the county boundary with Herefordshire. The surrounding countryside is very flat, so the hills – including Worcestershire Beacon, the high point – can be seen for miles around. The range is perhaps best known for its bottled spring water – which was first bottled and sold in the 1600s – earlier than almost anywhere else in the world. Great Malvern, at the foot of the hills, was the first place to bottle water on a commercial scale – something they did so well that it permeated all levels of society: Queen Elizabeth I allegedly refused to travel without a bottle at her side. The water also transformed the local area – Great Malvern's heyday was in the 19th century when it was a fashionable spa town, and visitors came from afar via the new railways. The secret is the hills themselves: formed from very hard rock, they do a superb job of filtering impurities from rainwater, which then flows from the numerous springs that dot the hills.

In a superb, full day I walked the entire length of the Malvern Hills (a round trip of some twenty kilometres), enjoying lovely views across Herefordshire, Worcestershire and beyond. They are however, very popular and I met many people on my walk. The Worcestershire high point walk is notable for being one of only two of my county high point walks which start at a railway station, the other being Derbyshire (Kinder Scout – accessible from Edale station, p100).

Start/parking: Great Malvern railway station

Satnav: WR14 3BX	**Start GR:** SO 783457	**High Point GR:** SO 768452
OS Map: Landranger 150 Worcester & The Malverns		
Distance: 4km	**Ascent:** 370m	**Time:** 2.5hrs

Cafe/Pub: The Blue Bird Tearooms, on Church Street in Great Malvern, is a good spot for tea after the walk (01684 561166). The St Ann's Well cafe, which you walk past on the route, is also a nice spot for tea.

Directions

Start from Great Malvern railway station.

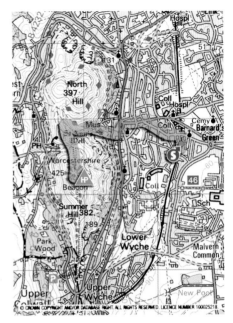

Turn N (right) out of the station. At the crossroads, turn W (left) and walk through the town for 800m up to the T-junction with the A449. Go just S of the junction and then take the path W for 500m to St Ann's Well, where there is a pleasant cafe. The route is tricky thereafter as there is a maze of paths, and the route is initially very steep. Head W for 400m and then S for 500m to the top. The top is a marble viewpoint, erected in commemoration of the death of Queen Victoria, with a trig point nearby.

For a superb full day of lovely views, you can continue S for up to 10km or so along the ridge of the Malvern Hills – highly recommended.

Nearby

The Malvern Hills were a particularly interesting place for me to visit as my great grandfather once lived in the area and painted the hills, and other Worcestershire scenes, over 100 years ago. Some of these paintings are now in the Bewdley Museum. At times on my walk it seemed that I was re-tracing his steps! www.wyreforestdc.gov.uk/museum

▲ LOOKING TOWARDS WALES FROM WORCESTERSHIRE BEACON

▲ HIGH CUP NICK, NEAR MICKLE FELL

Mickle Fell_#26

788m | 2,585ft   85th | 06/08/11 | solo

Yorkshire people are known for calling Yorkshire 'God's Country'. This may seem a bit over the top, but they do have a point. Yorkshire is a lovely county, with huge variety and many lovely places.

It is also a big county, by far the largest in England, ranging from the industrial towns in the south to the expanses of the Dales and the North Pennines. The historic cities of Sheffield, Leeds and York are here. The steep-sided industrial valleys near Halifax sit darkly in the west of the county, in stark contrast to the wonderful wild countryside of the Yorkshire Dales, the North York Moors and the North Pennines.

Yorkshire looms large in the history of Britain too: the Viking capital of York was here; the Wars of the Roses defined an era and the county's cities and coalfields powered much of the industrial revolution. And then there's Yorkshire's culture, which is even larger. Few other counties have such defined accents and attitudes or such a sense of identity.

Less defined, as with Lancashire, is the high point. The boundaries of Yorkshire have changed over the years and the historic top, Mickle Fell, is now in County Durham, replaced by the 736-metre Whernside in the Dales. Mickle Fell is in the North Pennines, a remote and bleak part of England. Quite featureless, their heathery, boggy terrain is largely without footpaths and is often described as 'England's last wilderness'. Neighbouring Cross Fell is actually one of the only places in the UK where the wind is so noted as to be named – the 'Helm Wind'.

Fittingly, this turned out to be one of my toughest walks. As I approached the summit of Mickle Fell, the weather closed in with a huge clap of thunder and a flash of lightning. A hasty retreat was made, only to find that Maize Beck, straightforward to cross just two hours previously, had swelled to a raging torrent! See page 23 for what happened next ... Notwithstanding all this, I found Yorkshire to be my favourite county in all of England.

Note: Mickle Fell is part of the Warcop Training Area on MOD land and access is heavily restricted. Part of the land is used as a firing range. Only two routes are permitted up Mickle Fell itself and access is limited to one designated weekend each month plus other specific times as available. Walkers have to obtain a numbered permit in advance – access details are available from the Warcop people on 0800 783 5181.

Start/parking: Hilton		
Satnav: CA16 6LU	**Start GR:** NY 734207	**High Point GR:** NY 805245
OS Map: Landranger 91 Appleby-in-Westmorland; Landranger 92 Barnard Castle & Richmond		
Distance: 20km	**Ascent:** 550m	**Time:** 10hrs
Cafe/Pub: Good tea and cakes at the Mulberry Bush cafe in nearby Kirkby Stephen. Britain's highest inn, the Tan Hill Inn (1,732 feet) is nearby, on the northern rim of the Yorkshire Dales.		

Directions

Start from the NE tip of Hilton, which is approx. 5km E of Appleby-in-Westmorland.

Take the bridleway NE; this starts in Hilton and is on the south side of Scordale Beck. Follow this E, then NE, then N, then NE along the length of Scordale for 5km, up to the valley head at Scordale Head. The bridleway becomes a footpath after approx. 3km and goes through an area of mine workings.

The path, which has hitherto been quite clear, becomes indistinct after Scordale Head as the land changes to boggy moorland, with tufty grass, heather and occasional peat hags to cross. This land is very remote and empty. Head NNE for 1km, then NE for 1km up to the right angle bend in Maize Beck. Then follow the S side of Maize Beck for 1km until you reach a wire fence which heads SSE up Mickle Fell. Follow the E side of this fence up Mickle Fell (this is the North Route in MoD terms) for 2km. At the top of the hill head NE for 500m to the cairn which marks the top of Mickle Fell.

Return via the same route. Note, if considering a different route, that it can be very difficult to cross Maize Beck after heavy rain (as I found to my cost). Plan for a long day, as the walk is 20km.

Nearby

Just north and west are, respectively, Cow Green Reservoir and High Cup Nick, two of the most noted water features in the county. The reservoir is worth a visit to see Cauldron Snout, the 'longest' waterfall in England. More like a steep and incredibly powerful set of rapids, it is a breath-taking sight. High Cup Nick, meanwhile, is an enormous, sheer-sided and crater-like valley, hewn from the hillside by a now-tiny waterfall. Both are well worth the walk!

MAIZE BECK, WHICH WE HAD TO CROSS IN FULL SPATE

ON THE WAY UP SCORDALE

▲ SWARTH BECK BEFORE THE RAINS

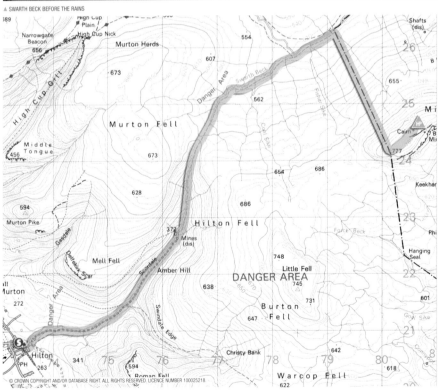

Whernside   *Gragareth*

736m | 2,415ft   28th and 29th | 12/09/08 | with Harry   627m | 2,057ft

The 1972 Local Government Act dramatically altered the counties of Britain. It aimed to standardise local government, making it simpler and more efficient, but in doing so abolished several counties and re-drew the boundaries of many others. This obviously caused confusion and, in some cases, upset amongst the inhabitants of those counties, who felt the loss of the county identity. (Many of the abolished counties still live on today in postal addresses, local papers and regional identities.)

Yorkshire and Lancashire got off lightly, with just a re-drawing of their boundaries. However, both lost their historic high points, which lie outside the new boundaries (see pages 254 and 148). Consequently, they have two 'new' tops – which lie near one another in the Yorkshire Dales National Park. Gragareth is modern-day Lancashire's high point, but is often overlooked in favour of the pre-1970s top, the Old Man of Coniston in the Lake District. Whernside, meanwhile, is recognised by some as Yorkshire's high point (under the new 1970s definition), while others prefer Mickle Fell (the high point under the pre-1970s definition). I decided to visit all four tops, and enjoyed my 'new' top walk so much that I have included it here.

The walk turned out to be a very long day (some 22 kilometres, actually the longest of any of my high point walks), longer than I had previously expected. It was, however, a lovely walk – the Yorkshire Dales are certainly hard to beat for scenery, and the landscape here is no exception. Defined by the limestone rock on which it sits, limestone can be seen at every turn: in the famous limestone 'pavements', in the small crags on the hills and in the impressive local caves (www.ingleboroughcave.co.uk). Numerous streams and rivers have cut deeply into the rock, creating impressive fissures and featured riverbeds. On our return route it was interesting to see the impressive Thornton Force and Pecca Falls – two of a number of waterfalls in the area. Indeed, Ingleton is famous for these waterfalls, which are among the most impressive in England.

Start/parking: Ingleton	**Satnav:** LA6 3HG	
Start GR: SD 694731	**High Point GR:** SD 738814 (Whernside); SD 687793 (Gragareth)	
OS Map: Landranger 98 Wensleydale & Upper Wharfedale		
Distance: 22km	**Ascent:** 750m	**Time:** 10.5hrs
Cafe/Pub: Lots of choice in Ingleton.		

Directions

Start in Ingleton.

Cross the bridge over the River Doe and take the road NNE up Oddie's Lane for 2km up to the path WNW to Twistleton Hall. Follow the road NW for 200m past the farm buildings and then head N up Twistleton Scar End along a footpath. This path goes NE for 4km to Ellerbeck, and would be tricky to navigate in mist. Continue NE to just past Bruntscar. Then head NNW up the side of Whernside for 1.2km; this gets increasingly steep until you reach the ridge. Follow the ridge NNE for 1km to the top of Whernside. The top is a trig point.

To continue to Gragareth, follow the path W for 1.5km down off Whernside as far as the road towards the head of Kingsdale; the second half of the descent is alongside a stone wall. Follow the road NNE for 500m as far as High Moss, then take the track NW and then W for 1.5km until its nearest point to Green Hill. Leave the track and go W for 500m up Green Hill. Follow the ridge SSW for 2.5km across boggy ground to the summit of Gragareth. The top is a trig point.

Continue S down the ridge until the intersection of two fences and then drop S down Dodson's Hill until reaching the Turbary Road path. Continue approx. 500m until reaching Blea Dubs. Then follow the track SSE for 1km until the road in Kingsdale. Follow the road across Kingsdale Beck and then, after 200m, take a path down to the river. Follow the path for 2km alongside River Twiss, past the impressive Thornton Force and Pecca Falls, down the woody track into Ingleton.

Nearby

On the Yorkshire side, visit the Wensleydale Creamery in Hawes, Gaping Gill (on the slopes of Ingleborough), or the spectacular Ribblehead Viaduct (as featured in *Harry Potter*). On the Lancashire side, visit Kirkby Lonsdale, a picturesque small town on the river Lune. The best bit of my Kirkby Lonsdale trip was undoubtedly to discover the Churchmouse Cheeses shop there; this was tremendous fun as the shopkeeper unexpectedly played a piano for his customers! Also nearby are the lovely, but not much visited, Bowland Fells and Lunedale.

▲ ON THE SUMMIT OF WHERNSIDE

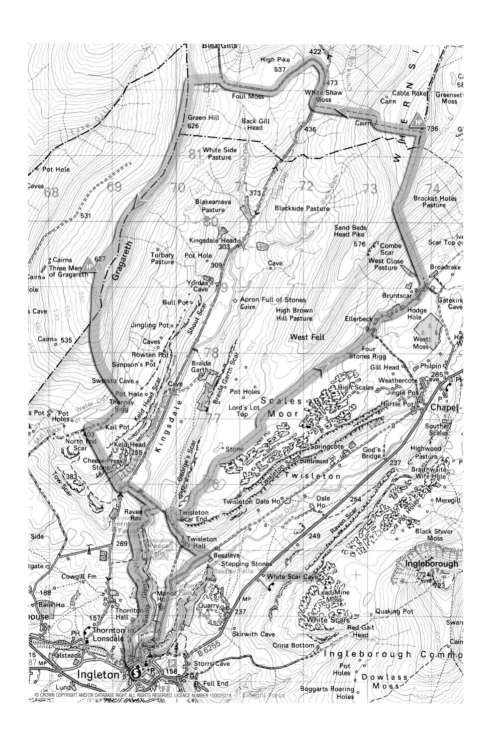

▲ LIMESTONE PAVEMENT, WITH WHERNSIDE IN THE DISTANCE

BY: ISTOCK

Holme Fen, Huntingdonshire

-3m | -9ft   06/09/08 | with Alex

If there is a high point, there must also be a low point! If I was going to visit the tops of the country, it seemed natural to visit the bottom too.

In Britain's case, this is Holme Fen, in Huntingdonshire (p132), which is nine feet below sea level. The low height is not natural, but the result of subsidence after the Whittlesey Mere wetlands were drained to create farmland. The low point is marked by the Holme Fen Posts, which came from London's Crystal Palace in the 19th century. When originally placed, their tops were level with the ground, to measure subsidence. They now stand four metres high!

The area had a spooky, unsafe feel to it on account of its remoteness, wetness and woods – so we were glad our stay was only for a short time. We came across just one other person while we were there.

Start/parking: Verge of minor road which goes through the Holme Fen National Nature Reserve

Satnav: PE7 3PT (nearest)	Start GR: TL 202893	High Point GR: TL 202893

OS Map: Landranger 142 Peterborough

Distance: 0.5km	Ascent: N/A	Time: 0.5hrs

Cafe/Pub: Try The Bell, in nearby Stilton. (01733 241066, www.thebellstilton.co.uk).

Directions

Start near the Holme Fen Posts on the verge of the minor road which goes through the Holme Fen National Nature Reserve. This is alongside Holme Lode ditch, 2km NE of Holme. Holme is 10km S of Peterborough.

Follow the track from the road for 100m, over Holme Lode ditch and to the Holme Fen Posts. These mark Great Britain's low point. The posts, which come from London's 19th century Crystal Palace, were exposed after Whittlesey Mere was drained and the ground sank.

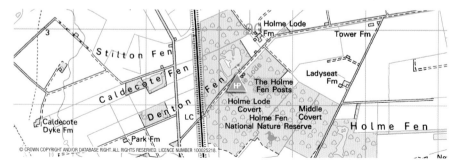

▲ HOLME LODE, NEXT TO THE LOW POINT

About the author

Mark Clarke's interest in hill walking started when he was at school and took part in the Duke of Edinburgh Award scheme. As part of this and other school activities, he made several visits to Snowdonia, culminating in his Gold Award expedition over four days and fifty miles – following in the footsteps of his two brothers and in the process pulling off the perhaps unusual feat of three brothers each achieving the Gold Award.

The mountain skills and disciplines which he had learnt in Snowdonia sat idle for many years subsequently, but happily stood him in good stead on his *High Point* project – he even used the very same compass which he had used in Snowdonia some forty years earlier.

He has a MA from Oxford University and is a Fellow of the Institute of Chartered Accountants. Until 2008 his career was in the financial services and management consultancy sectors and in Whitehall. Since then, he has taken up a variety of part time non-executive roles in business and not for profit organisations.

Mark lives in London with his wife of over thirty years, Alex, and has three children, all of whom are now in their twenties.